THE ALEISTER CROWLEY MANUAL

THE ALEISTER CROWLEY MANUAL

Thelemic Magick for Modern Times

MARCO VISCONTI

WATKINS
1893

This edition first published in the UK and USA in 2023 by
Watkins, an imprint of Watkins Media Limited
Unit 11, Shepperton House
89–93 Shepperton Road
London
N1 3DF

enquiries@watkinspublishing.com

Design and typography copyright © Watkins Media Limited 2023

Text copyright © Marco Visconti
Internal images and diagrams by Mars Neumann

Marco Visconti has asserted his right under the Copyright, Designs
and Patents Act 1988 to be identified as the author of this work.

10 9 8 7 6 5 4 3 2 1

Designed and typeset by JCS Publishing Services Ltd

Printed and bound in the United Kingdom by TJ Books Limited
A CIP record for this book is available from the British Library

ISBN: 978-1-78678-736-1 (Hardback)
ISBN: 978-1-78678-737-8 (eBook)

www.watkinspublishing.com

CONTENTS

nanos gigantum humeris insidentes

(Bernard of Chartres, 12th century)

FOREWORD

FOREWORD

Thelemic magick!

In 1967, as a teenager in the Bronx, I was obsessed with ceremonial magic. My only resource at the time was A E Waite's *The Book of Ceremonial Magic*, sometimes called *The Book of Black Magic and of Pacts*. Waite had a very negative, even hostile, perspective on the grimoires and this oozes like ichor throughout his work. An initiate of the Golden Dawn, like Aleister Crowley, his contrarian position on magic was bizarre to say the least, but his was the only book I knew of at the time that laid it all out: magic circles, instruments, demons and angels, incenses, occult calendars, lengthy incantations, and the rest. It seemed like it was all there but actually it was missing some essential elements, such as the basic training required of a prospective magician. Waite criticized the grimoires' eclectic approach to religion, the crazy mixture of Christianity and Judaism, the garbled and mangled words in Hebrew, Latin and Greek, yet offered little to no guidance as to how the grimoires should be (or could be) used. He actually had been trained in ritual magic and in initiation but in this book contributed little or nothing to those who would have benefited most from this education.

I used it anyway.

Between awkward rituals at night in Pelham Bay Park with robes and swords and Gloria incense, and scary, table-tipping séances on Revere Avenue, I was making some headway and producing some phenomena, but there were lacunae in my understanding (to put it mildly). Then, one afternoon in the basement of Samuel Weiser's Bookstore south of Union Square in Manhattan, I came across a book entitled – most helpfully – *Magick in Theory and Practice*. It was published by Castle Books, and its author's name was the appropriately spooky-sounding Aleister Crowley. 'This', I said to myself, 'is exactly what I need! A book that will take me through all the basic steps to occult attainment.'

Yeah, right.

The many references to Golden Dawn concepts, yogic practices, Egyptian religion, and citations of Crowley's own works, went right over my head. I had no earthly idea what he was on about. But his tone … that was something else. He made the practice of ritual magic seem reasonable, seem based on scientific principles, and he wrote as if he knew what he was talking about. That alone was a revelation. He was a modern, not an ancient. His language was clear, even if his references were too arcane for me to grasp. He was in command of this subject in ways that no other writer I had come across in my 16–17 years on Earth at the time could match. I was sold. I began the painstaking process of deconstructing Crowley to the extent that I could begin to apply his instructions to my own experiments.

But … but what if there had been a book available to me at the time that was a real introduction to the subject of ceremonial magic, moreover one from the modern Crowley, a Thelemic, perspective? A book to explain Crowley's book explaining magic? It would have saved me a lot of time, and a lot of money, and probably some pieces of what I laughingly refer to as my 'soul'.

Today we have a plethora of pundits on social media, on video sites, and in what bookstores remain, claiming all sorts of knowledge in this field. From my perspective of more than 50 years studying these arcane arts I can state with a high degree of confidence that they are mostly poseurs and posturers. 'Occulture' has become more of an online literary/ arts experience and hangout for armchair theorizers than a subterranean demi-monde of serious occult practitioners.

As the occult becomes trendy, the field is inundated by 'influencers' and professional witches, shamans, and the like, and someone new to the study is easily confused and, often, cheated by these carnival barkers.

Part of the problem lies with the orders themselves and the so-called secret societies that have pimped out their rituals, their initiations, and their reputations in what seem to me to be desperate attempts to become and remain 'relevant' even though that was never the aim or the purpose of magicians in the past. Another aspect of the problem is that social media is an ego machine, and the need to one-up one's competitors with the *mot juste* or the scathing put-down is just too tempting for newcomers to resist. There is also the rather painful attempt by some authors to make occultism seem folksy and harmless, with heavy doses of sophomoric humour, word play, and over-familiar references to sacred texts within an irrelevant pop cultural context. By the way, if you're doing it right, your occultism does have the potential to cause harm.

Finally, and perhaps most importantly, there is no baseline for determining the spiritual attainments of another human being. It is too easy to claim all sorts of advanced degrees (in the orders) or deep insights and accomplishments (among the independent practitioners) without having to offer proof of any kind of deeper knowledge or ability. With the rising popularity of Thelema – the philosophical system developed by Crowley – it has become too easy for some of his followers to adopt a pose of smug superiority, spiritual arrogance, and sarcastic omniscience in imitation of Crowley's pompous literary style if not his genuine mystical insights.

Whereas in 1967 I had no options other than Waite and Crowley's *Magick in Theory and Practice*, today there are way too many options, too many voices crying for attention in a field that once was identified by the slogan: *To know, to will, to dare, to keep silent*. One weeps for the serious, sober neophyte of today who feels drawn to this subject and its rigorous practices but who becomes side-tracked by social media adepts.

Well, until now.

There are a number of books out there that will take one through some basics where ceremonial magic is concerned, but very few that clarify the role Thelema plays in magic. And there are books that discuss Thelema from various angles, but which do not focus on the actual practice of magic even though it was an intense discipleship in magic that led Crowley to discover Thelema. It is also common for people to regard Thelema as a kind of religion in its own right, a stand-alone philosophy that requires total belief and fealty to Crowley's written word, but Crowley himself despised that type of mentality. If Thelema as a religion demands self-empowerment (as it seems to do) then it is already a different animal than the faiths that preceded it that demanded (and still demand) blind obedience. And how does one empower oneself in a religious or spiritual context?

Magic.

Magic is a technology. It uses the tools of consciousness, of the senses and the mechanisms of the body and the body mind interface, to cause change to occur. It is, as Crowley said, both a science and an art. That is not a throwaway line. It is actually quite profound in its implications.

What Marco Visconti has done is to apply that understanding to an instructional text that can be used by anyone on the magical or the Thelemic path. For the aspiring magician, his book clarifies what has to be done by the individual in order to prepare body and mind for the rituals that will follow. For the Thelemite, his book explains Thelema from the magical perspective. This is the book I wish had existed in the 1960s when I was struggling with Waite and Crowley in equal measure. Crowley wrote[1] that in the new aeon (or 'new age', the one we

---

[1] Crowley, A, *Magick in Theory and Practice*, Dover, New York, 1976, p 237.

have already entered) using an outdated form of magic was like using a boomerang in a firefight. Compare Mr Visconti's text with the *Key of Solomon* or any of the other medieval and later grimoires and you will note the differences immediately. The same basic procedures are described and expanded upon, but in new and unexpected ways.

And Visconti knows whereof he speaks and writes. He comes from a long background in Thelema and magick and has been conducting classes in the grimoires. His command of the subject matter and his ability to describe and explain even the most arcane references is without equal, in my estimation. There is no bombast in his work, no sly evasions or gnomic allusions. This is a practical text, written by a practising magician, for other practising magicians. And it is all within a Thelemic context that I found both educational and at times illuminating.

Okay, I've gone on long enough. It's time you see for yourself what I mean. If you are already on the path, this book is an excellent *vade mecum* to take with you on the way. If you are new, you arc in luck. This is the place to start. Don't be like 1967 me. Take a deep breath (Marco shows you how) and begin!

Peter Levenda

INTRODUCTION

INTRODUCTION

I will start by sharing a secret with you: I really don't like writing about magick. I am firmly in the camp of those who insist that magick is strictly an experiential affair.

Yes, it is fundamental to study the philosophy and theology behind it (oh no, we are already touching on the subject of religion, aren't we). But often, one gets bogged down trying to grasp 'all that there is' and simply never starts doing magick. You may have heard the term 'armchair magician' to denote those who read about magick but never practise it. There is an excellent novel by Susanna Clarke, *Jonathan Strange & Mr Norrell*, which uses this conundrum as its central plot device. I definitely suggest you read it if you haven't. I am a Jonathan Strange much more than I am a Mr Norrell – the one who dares to actually use these rituals instead of simply philosophizing about them ad infinitum. I hope you will be too by the end of this book.

DO WHAT THOU WILT SHALL BE THE WHOLE OF THE LAW

This is one of the three central aphorisms of Thelema, a Western esoteric and occult social or spiritual philosophy and new religious movement founded in the early 1900s by Aleister Crowley, the notorious English writer, mystic, occultist, and all-around polymath. The word Thelema is the English transliteration of the koine Greek noun θέλημα, 'will', from the verb θέλω (*thélō*): 'to will, wish, want or purpose'. The other two

WHY THE TITLE?

Initially, I wanted to call this book *Thelema After Tears*. That's because you are likely to shed plenty of those if you try to approach this esoteric philosophy the way Aleister Crowley himself presented it to the public, especially in his magnum opus *Liber ABA: Magick in Theory and Practice*. Despite spending quite some time in the introduction insisting that his book was written for everyone, '... to help the Banker, the Pugilist, the Biologist, the Poet, the Navvy, the Grocer, the Factory Girl, the Mathematician, the Stenographer, the Golfer, the Wife, the Consul – and all the rest – to fulfil themselves perfectly, each in his or her own proper function', the final result is something that requires years of experience and knowledge of the subject matter to truly be appreciated. The Edwardian prose doesn't help, either. However, my editor also convinced me that we needed something catchier and that the name of the Beast himself would do the trick. And so here you get *The Aleister Crowley Manual*, a step-by-step primer that, maybe, Uncle Al himself would have loved reading as a total beginner!

aphorisms are 'Love is the law, love under will' and 'Every man and every woman is a star', but we'll get back to these later.

Magick begins with 'doing', and after almost three entire decades of calling myself a magician, I am still convinced that it's the doing that must be at the core of magical practice. Else, it's 'just' philosophy or theology. So the book that is now in your hands will focus first and foremost on all the things you can 'do' to be a magician. We will still have to go a bit deeper in places so that you can get a good early understanding of the reasons why

we practise these rituals and techniques. I will try to keep that
to a minimum.

With this promise, I am setting some boundaries as well
This book is aimed at those just getting started on the path of
ceremonial magick, primarily as codified at the turn of the 20th
century by the Hermetic Order of the Golden Dawn[2] first and
then by Aleister Crowley.

However, by setting these boundaries, I am already clarifying
that this is very much a beginner's book. I simplify things here
and there, and the overall approach is incredibly syncretic and
eclectic. If you tend to have a purist approach to what you study,
you will likely not gel very much with how I present these ideas
and these practices. Still, let me try to win you over, giving you
a little perspective. At the very end of the book, I provide a
reading list for those who will want to delve even deeper.

HOW THIS BOOK CAME TO BE

I am writing this introduction in May 2022 ev.[3] More than
two years have passed since the beginning of the COVID-19
pandemic, which changed our lives forever. When the lockdowns
started, going back to the early days of my magical training
helped immensely, and I realized it was something I could give

---

[2] The Hermetic Order of the Golden Dawn (Latin: *Ordo Hermeticus Aurorae
   Aureae*), more commonly the Golden Dawn (*Aurora Aurea*), was a secret
   society devoted to the study and practice of the occult, metaphysics, and
   paranormal activities during the late 19th and early 20th centuries. Known
   as a magical order, the Hermetic Order of the Golden Dawn was active in
   Great Britain and focused its practices on theurgy and spiritual development.
   Many present-day concepts of ritual and magic that are at the centre of
   contemporary traditions, such as Wicca and Thelema, were inspired by the
   Golden Dawn, which became one of the largest single influences on 20th
   century Western occultism. (*Wikipedia*)

[3] *Era Vulgaris*, Crowley's replacement for AD/CE.

to others to help them too. So I bought a Zoom subscription, organized a Patreon community, and taught magick, the spiritual evolutionary practice of the West. We spent the lockdown years meeting online, at times twice a week. We organized lectures, seminars, and even rituals. We scried the Enochian aethyrs, and we conjured the Olympic spirits of the *Arbatel*. As I write these words, we are still doing it, though the frequency has diminished since the world reopened.

This book is what came out of those lessons.

To really level up with this practice, you do not need fancy tools or robes or the marble halls of a gilded temple. Yes, those things might become useful at some point down the line. But to start the alchemical process that will turn your lead into gold, all you need is a quiet room and the perseverance to keep going to the end.

And that is a bit trickier than it might sound at first, as we all live hectic lives in increasingly smaller spaces. But if you are genuinely willing to invest in this experience, then this practice is truly for everyone: busy working mums, retired people, younger social media influencers, and everyone in-between.

This book has a simple, structured process to help you stay on track: each chapter is a lesson meant to be read and practised for a month. Each month you will learn several new tools to add to your magical arsenal.

The benefits gained from bringing magick into your life are manifold: a deeper understanding of our role in the universe, the ability to communicate with the other, and gaining wisdom and insight from such relationships. What you will gain from these practices is a new and more profound sense of awareness of your own role in the universe.

Some call it 'True Will'.

TRUE WILL? WHAT'S THAT?

In Thelema, True Will (also Pure Will) is defined as a moment-to-moment path of action that operates in perfect harmony with everything else. True Will does not equate with conscious intent. Rather it signifies the interplay between the most profound self – using this term very loosely – and the entire universe. This is a fundamental point since it single-handedly dissolves any solipsistic reading of this concept. In a nutshell, 'Do what thou wilt' does NOT mean 'do whatever you want'.

To discover one's True Will means to have eliminated or bypassed false desires, conflicts, and habits. It also implies access to a direct connection with the divine. At this point, one acts in alignment with nature, just as a stream flows downhill, with neither resistance nor 'lust of result' (outside motivations).

A crucial step toward this goal is to learn to overcome any socially derived inhibitions. For Crowley, this was done mainly through rejecting the appeals to modesty and the fear of sexuality that highlight the Christian worldview. This reappropriation of the sensual and sexual experience is further codified in the **Knowledge and Conversation of the Holy Guardian Angel** – where *knowledge* is very much intended as carnal, even if consumed on subtler planes of existence.

ENTER THE HGA

I realize I started this chapter by saying there won't be much theory. Still, we must establish some critical concepts before we start *doing* magick.

HGA stands for – you guessed it – **Holy Guardian Angel**. This is possibly one of the most misunderstood concepts in the history of magick.

Those who wrote about it define it in a thousand different ways and never seem to agree on what its nature really is.

Let's be clear: we are not talking of an actual 'angel' here. We will learn about what angels are later on and how to invoke and work with them. But the HGA is not one of them. Instead, it can be seen as the equivalent of **The Higher and Divine Genius** of the Hermetic Order of the Golden Dawn, the ***Augoeides*** of Iamblichus, the ***Atman*** of Hinduism, and the ***Daimon*** of the ancient Greeks.

When composing *Magick Without Tears* in his late 60s, Crowley states that the Holy Guardian Angel is not one's 'self' but a discrete and independent being.

In my time, I came to understand it as an expression of God – whatever you consider God to be. In *Liber LXV*, one of the most essential Holy Books of Thelema (the core 'inspired' texts that contain the doctrine of the whole magical philosophy), the name of the HGA is given as Adonai, which is Hebrew for 'The Lord'.

So, how do we manifest this 'Knowledge and Conversation'? First, it's fundamental we establish, right here and now, that there isn't a single way to do so common to everyone. In *One Star In Sight*, Crowley writes:

> It is impossible to lay down precise rules by which a man may attain to the knowledge and conversation of His Holy Guardian Angel; for that is the particular secret of each one of us; a secret not to be told or even divined by any other, whatever his grade. It is the Holy of Holies, whereof each man is his own High Priest, and none knoweth the name of his brother's God, or the Rite that invokes Him.[4]

---

[4] Apologies for the gendered language: I elected not to modify the few quotes I will use throughout the book for precision's sake.

However, what can be done is to learn to lay solid foundations for this Holy of Holies he describes. By building your own **magical pyramid** you become aware of the flux of energy, recognizing and refining the elements (Fire, Earth, Air, and Water) within and without, and finally by unlocking that quintessence[5] that is the first link to the divine.

THE GREAT WORK

This lifelong process is called the **Great Work**, or **magnum opus** in Latin. Magick is one of the tools used during this process. Its goal is to unify the microcosm and the macrocosm, bringing together all the polarities in opposition that create our perceived reality.

The ability to accomplish the Great Work requires much preparation and effort. Therefore, this book will focus on some of its key elements: familiarity with the Hermetic Qabalah (especially the Tree of Life, which lays out a map of reality and a system of correspondences), disciplined concentration (meditation), the development of one's **body of light** (to experience other planes, as well as having a better perception of the physical one) and the constant and regular invocation of specific deities or spiritual beings.

You can consider the Great Work as the conscious process of spiritual growth. By consciously committing to this long path and sealing oneself within one's own 'alchemical vessel', the inner heat of psychic struggle generated from this aids in the dissolution of ego boundaries and the integration of the many polarities battling with each other.

---

[5]   Literally, the 'fifth essence', the supposed substance of which heavenly bodies are composed.

It's important to notice how fitting is the alchemical allegory here: as the precursors of today's chemists tried to turn base lead into glorious gold, toiling away in their laboratories for months and months on end, so the magicians have worked since time immemorial to transmute their humanity back into the original, forgotten divine nature.

HIGH OR LOW MAGICK?

Some of you may already be familiar with these ideas. Indeed, yoga (at least a very mainstream version) is more popular than ever with everyone, from occultists to soccer moms. And in recent years, witchcraft and sigil magick have become relatively well known.

What we are doing here is to lay the foundations for what's usually known as **high magick**, or **theurgy**. We are becoming first aware and then in control of our more rarefied wavelengths of consciousness as we become close to the divine spark at the core of our very being. You can think of it as a vertical spiritual evolution: the Great Work realized.

The spells of witchcraft, the sigil magick of results, and even the simple manifestation mantras of the new age are more akin to what I call **low magick** or **sorcery**. A kind of horizontal expansion, if you will.

Using terms like high or low might lend to thinking one is better than the other. In fact, the magician truly should master both to fully be able to call themselves an adept. However, the focus of these lessons is squarely on the theurgy side of things.

OK, BUT WHAT IS MAGICK?!

Crowley provided various different definitions of this term over his career.

The most popular is likely 'the science and art of causing change to occur in conformity with Will'.

Immediately you can notice that he describes it as the union of science and art: the rational and the inspired. Crowley was living in a time when science was finally starting to fully explain the world around him, so he wanted a piece of that. But he also wanted to retain the artist's creative impulse without sacrificing the whole of the human experience on the altar of cold logic. Furthermore, the term Will (with a capital W) assumes a specific meaning in his system of esoteric philosophy, Thelema. We will analyze this in full in a later chapter, but for now, remember that the Will is a goal, not a starting point.

It should be noted that in a letter to his disciple Karl Germer, Crowley stated: 'Magick is getting into communication with individuals who exist on a higher plane than ours. Mysticism is the raising of oneself to their level.'

The nature of these beings, the intertwining of magick and mystic practices, and the result of these communications, are at the very core of the magician's experience.

THE NEXT STEPS

It's time to start our journey. Our destination is Heliopolis, the City of the Sun that the Egyptians called ON. We will also build our inner temple, or magical pyramid, as we travel toward it.

We'll start from the foundations: learning to breathe consciously, acknowledging the four hermetic elements, and striving to be present at all times.

We will then erect the superstructure: understanding the power of the mantra, learning the pentagram and middle pillar rituals, and accessing the astral plane.

In time, we will build it up to the very pinnacle. Therein, we will unlock the quintessence, complete the pentagram practice and begin the hexagram work.

There, and only there, we will start looking at what Thelema really means in practice.

AS ABOVE
SO BELOW:
THE LEXICON OF
CORRESPONDENCES

CHAPTER 1

AS ABOVE SO BELOW:
THE LEXICON OF
CORRESPONDENCES

One of the earliest attempts to create a manual of practical magick made by Aleister Crowley is a short text that first appeared in *The Equinox 1.2* in 1909. Titled *Liber O vel Manus et Sagittae sub figurâ VI*, it begins with an important reminder for everyone embarking on studying this discipline.

Crowley tells us that the student will learn of the sephiroth and the paths, of spirits and conjurations; of gods, spheres, planes, and many other things **which may or may not exist.**

And immediately doubles down by saying that it doesn't really matter whether these exist or not. Once again, the focus should be strictly put on the *doing*. By doing certain things, specific results will follow without fail. Finally, Crowley concludes by insisting that students are most earnestly warned against attributing objective reality or philosophic validity to any of them. In a nutshell, one should avoid constantly asking why or how certain things happen. Instead, by experimenting with magick, notice how control over one's mind expands, and the horizons of what's possible become broader and more expansive.

MAGICAL AND MYTHICAL THINKING

A few years later, he would greatly expand on all these ideas and pen his magnum opus: *Liber ABA*. Over the years, it has become known by the title of its *Part III, Magick in Theory and Practice*, or simply *Magick*.

In chapter 8 of part III, he says that the whole subject of magick is an example of **mythopoeia** (myth-making) in that particular form called **disease of language**. By that, he refers to the basic human (aka uninitiated) need to 'make sense' of everything through rational explanation so that we can communicate it using our language. He goes on by telling us that the old name for ritual, 'grimoire' (from the French *grammaire*), in truth only refers to the grammar (that is, the unspoken rules) of the universe.

And here's the lesson: magick is a kind of alphabet and symbol set comprised of a series of conventions.

Our language – indeed, our consciousness, which employs language – is a form of disease because consciousness reflects reality to us and distorts the image. We don't see our actual inclinations (True Will) because we're distracted by mental phenomena such as self-image.

So we turn to magick and its rituals, using the aid of one kind of make-believe to break through the veil of make-believe that our consciousness has used to bind us. Magick can thus be a potent weapon in the right hands.

It's now time to introduce the concept of 'magical correspondences'.

KABBALAH OR QABALAH?

The Hermetic Order of the Golden Dawn was partly an expression of Hermetic Qabalah, derived from Jewish mystical Kabbalah. The different spelling, with the Q or the K, implies a profound difference between the two approaches.

Kabbalah, a type of Torah interpretation in Judaism, gained prominence in the 16th century via the publication of the *Zohar*. As offspring of the true God, Israel is said to represent the *shekinah*, or presence, in the universe. It also introduced the decreasing four worlds: Atziluth, the world of emanation; Briah, the world of creation; Yetzirah, the world of formation; and finally Assiah, the world of action. It postulated God as the transcendent Ain Soph (prior to manifestation), and – most famously – the ten sephiroth of the Tree of Life as the universe's blueprint. It accomplished this by reading the text's explicit ethics.

Esoteric societies drew from Christian Kabbalah from the 15th century to the Enlightenment. These ideas were practised and reinterpreted by occultists such Heinrich Cornelius Agrippa, Pico Della Mirandola, and Éliphas Lévi before becoming famous in modern esoterica.

We shall employ a 'Westernized' form of the mystical system – Qabalah with a Q – as a tool for our magical training. It focuses primarily on the ten sephiroth or 'emanations' of the godhead, which are arranged in a symbol called the Tree of Life. These can also be viewed as levels of a heavenly ladder leading from Earth to godhead – as a map of reality. Gematria is a further practical application of Qabalah. Isopsephy, which uses the Greek alphabet instead of the 22 letters of the Hebrew script, is a related technique to gematria.

Let me give you an example:

Will = *Thelema*: Θελημα = 9 + 5 + 30 + 8 + 40 + 1 = 93
Love = *Agape*: Αγαπη = 1 + 3 + 1 + 80 + 8 = 93

There is a secret sympathy of meaning between the words *thelema* and *agape* because they both enumerate to 93. Hence, Thelema is known as the '93 current'.

'Like produces like' is how Sir James George Frazer, the author of *The Golden Bough*, summarized the sympathetic magic theory.

Frazer subsequently divided the concept into two separate components known as the Law of Similarity and the Law of Contact/Contagion. He said:

> From the first of these principles, namely the Law of Similarity, the magician infers that he can produce any effect he desires merely by imitating it: from the second he infers that whatever he does to a material object will affect equally the person with whom the object was once in contact, whether it formed part of his body or not.

The *Emerald Tablet of Hermes Trismegistus* is considered the earliest example of this mythical thinking, especially in the famous aphorism:

> That which is below is like that which is above and that which is above is like that which is below to do the miracles of one only thing.

THE TREE OF LIFE: A MAP OF REALITY

Liber 777 is Crowley's attempt at summarizing the entirety of Qabalah's teachings and system of correspondences, focusing on the glyph called the **Tree of Life**.

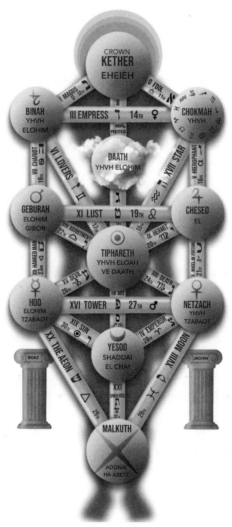

Above: The Tree of Life

The title relates to a lightning flash descending the diagrammatic worlds, the zigzag pattern implying three declining 7s, and the sum value of the gematria of the paths. It consists of around 191 columns, with each row matching to a single sephirah or path on the Tree of Life for a total of 35 rows, and is used for rapid reference for correlating mnemonics and religious aspects for use in magick.

In this book, I decided to present you with a reduced number of tables, with enough information to get you started and to complete the practices you will find through its pages. If you decide to get serious with magick, however, I definitely suggest you acquire a copy of *Liber 777* and study it in its entirety. Nowadays, you can find plenty of other texts that aim at recreating a coherent system of correspondences. James A Eshelman's *776½: Tables for Practical Ceremonial* and Stephen Skinner's *The Complete Magician's Tables* are fantastic in their own right.

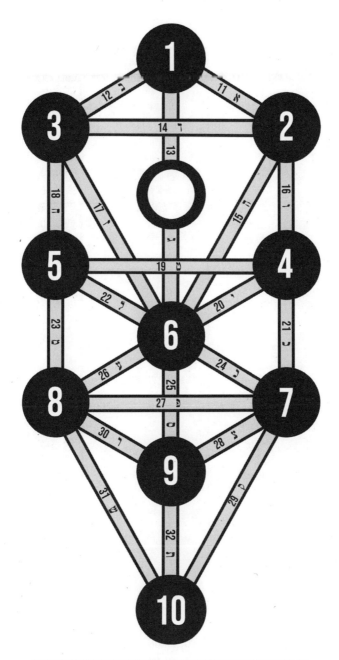

THIS ARRANGEMENT IS THE BASIS OF THE WHOLE SYSTEM OF THE FOLLOWING PAGES

Above and following pages: Table of correspondences adapted from Aleister Crowley's *Liber 777*

KEY SCALE	I HEBREW NAMES		II ENGLISH INTERPRETATION	III THE HEAVENS
0	אין	AIN	NOTHING	
	אין סוף	AIN SOPH	NO LIMIT	
	אין סוף אור	AIN SOPH AUR	LIMITLESS L.V.X	
1	כתר	KETHER	CROWN	SPHERE OF PRIMUM MOBILE
2	חכמה	CHOKMAH	WISDOM	SPHERE OF THE ZODIAC
3	בינה	BINAH	UNDERSTANDING	SPHERE OF SATURN
4	כסד	CHESED	MERCY	SPHERE OF JUPITER
5	גבורה	GEBURAH	STRENGTH	SPHERE OF MARS
6	תפארת	TIPHARETH	BEAUTY	SPHERE OF SOL
7	נצה	NETZACH	VICTORY	SPHERE OF VENUS
8	הוד	HOD	SPLENDOUR	SPHERE OF MERCURY
9	יסוד	YESOD	FOUNDATION	SPHERE OF LUNA
10	מלכות	MALKUTH	KINGDOM	SPHERE OF THE ELEMENTS
11	אלף	ALEPH	OX	AIR
12	בית	BETH	HOUSE	MERCURY
13	גמל	GIMEL	CAMEL	LUNA
14	דלת	DALETH	DOOR	VENUS
15	הה	HÉ	WINDOW	ARIES △
16	וו	VAU	NAIL	TAURUS ▽
17	זין	ZAIN	SWORD	GEMINI
18	חית	CHETH	FENCE	CANCER ▽
19	טית	TETH	SERPENT	LEO △
20	יוד	YOD	HAND	VIRGO ▽
21	כף	KAPH	PALM	JUPITER
22	למד	LAMED	OX GOAD	LIBRA △
23	מים	MAIM	WATER	WATER
24	כון	NUN	FISH	SCORPIO ▽
25	סמך	SAMEKH	PROP	SAGITTARIUS
26	עין	AYIN	EYE	CAPRICORN ▽
27	פה	PÉ	MOUTH	MARS
28	צדי	TZADDI	FISH HOOK	AQUARIUS △
29	קוף	QOPH	BACK OF HEAD	PISCES ▽
30	ריש	RESH	HEAD	SOL
31	שין	SHIN	TOOTH	FIRE
32	תו	TAU	TAU (AS EGYPTIAN)	SATURN
32 BIS	תו	TAU		EARTH
31 BIS	שין	SHIN		SPIRIT

KEY SCALE	IV THE SWORD & THE SERPENT	V MYSTIC NUMBERS OF THE SEPHIROTH	VI GENERAL TAROT ATTRIBUTION
0		0	
1		1	THE 4 ACES
2		3	THE 4 TWOS - KINGS/KNIGHTS
3		6	THE 4 THREES - QUEENS
4		10	THE 4 FOURS
5		15	THE 4 FIVES
6		21	THE 4 SIXES
7		28	THE 4 SEVENS
8		36	THE 4 EIGHTS
9		45	THE 4 NINES
10		55	THE 4 TENS - EMPRESSES/PRINCESSES
11		66	THE FOOL (SWORD) EMPERORS/PRINCES
12		78	THE JUGGLER
13		91	THE HIGH PRIESTESS
14		105	THE EMPRESS
15		120	THE EMPEROR
16		136	THE HIEROPHANT
17		153	THE LOVERS
18		171	THE CHARIOT
19		190	STRENGTH
20		210	HERMIT
21		231	WHEEL OF FORTUNE
22		253	JUSTICE
23		276	THE HANGED MAN - (CUPS) QUEENS
24		300	DEATH
25		325	TEMPERANCE
26		351	THE DEVIL
27		378	THE HOUSE OF GOD
28		406	THE STAR
29		435	THE MOON
30		465	THE SUN
31		496	JUDGEMENT (WANDS) KINGS/KNIGHTS
32		528	THE UNIVERSE
32 BIS			EMPRESSES (COINS)
31 BIS			ALL 22 TRUMPS

Column IV (THE SWORD & THE SERPENT) vertical text:

THE FLAMING SWORD FOLLOWS THE DOWNWARD COURSE OF THE SEPHIROTH, AND IS COMPARED TO THE LIGHTNING FLASH. ITS HILT IS IN KETHER AND ITS POINT IN MALKUTH.

THE SERPENT OF WISDOM FOLLOWS THE COURSE OF THE PATHS OR LETTERS UPWARDS, ITS HEAD BEING THUS IN א ITS TAIL IN ת. א, מ AND ש ARE THE MOTHER LETTERS, REFERRING TO THE ELEMENTS; ב, ג, ד, כ, פ, ר, AND ת, THE DOUBLE LETTERS, TO THE PLANETS; THE REST, SINGLE LETTERS, TO THE ZODIAC.

KEY SCALE	VII KING SCALE OF COLOUR י	VIII QUEEN SCALE OF COLOUR ה	IX EMPEROR SCALE OF COLOUR ו	X EMPRESS SCALE OF COLOUR ה
0				
1	BRILLIANCE	WHITE BRILLIANCE	WHITE BRILLIANCE	WHITE FLECKED GOLD
2	PURE SOFT BLUE	GREY	BLUE PEARL GREY	WHITE FLECKED RED, BLUE, YELLOW
3	CRIMSON	BLACK	DANK BROWN	GREY FLECKED PINK
4	DEEP VIOLET	BLUE	DEEP PURPLE	DEEP AZURE FLECKED YELLOW
5	ORANGE	SCARLET RED	BRIGHT SCARLET	RED FLECKED BLACK
6	CLEAR PINK ROSE	YELLOW	RICH SALMON	GOLD AMBER
7	AMBER	EMERALD	BRIGHT YELLOW GREEN	OLIVE FLECKED GOLD
8	VIOLET PURPLE	ORANGE	RED-RUSSET	YELLOW-BROWN FLECKED WHITE
9	INDIGO	VIOLET	VERY DARK PURPLE	CITRINE FLECKED AZURE
10	YELLOW	CITRINE+OLIVE+RUSSET+BLACK	AS QUEEN SCALE, FLECKED GOLD	BLACK RAYED YELLOW
11	BRIGHT PALE YELLOW	SKY BLUE	BLUE EMERALD GREEN	EMERALD FLECKED GOLD
12	YELLOW	PURPLE	GREY	INDIGO RAYED VIOLET
13	BLUE	SILVER	COLD PALE BLUE	SILVER RAYED SKY-BLUE
14	EMERALD GREEN	SKY BLUE	EARLY SPRING GREEN	BRIGHT ROSE OF CERISE RAYED PALE YELLOW
15	SCARLET	RED	BRILLIANT FLAME	GLOWING RED
16	RED ORANGE	DEEP INDIGO	DEEP WARM OLIVE	RICH BROWN
17	ORANGE	PALE MAUVE	NEW YELLOW LEATHER	REDDISH GREY INCLINED TO MAUVE
18	AMBER	MAROON	RIGH BRIGHT RUSSET	DARK GREENISH BROWN
19	YELLOW, GREENISH	DEEP PURPLE	GREY	REDDISH AMBER
20	GREEN, YELLOWISH	SLATE GREY	GREEN GREY	PLUM COLOUR
21	VIOLET	BLUE	RICH PURPLE	BRIGHT BLUE RAYED YELLOW
22	EMERALD GREEN	BLUE	DEEP BLUE-GREEN	PALE GREEN
23	DEEP PURPLE	SEA GREEN	DEEP OLIVE-GREEN	WHITE FLECKED PURPLE
24	GREEN BLUE	DULL BROWN	VERY DARK BROWN	LIVID INDIGO BROWN
25	BLUE	YELLOW	GREEN	DARK VIVID BLUE
26	INDIGO	BLACK	BLUE BLACK	COLD DARK GREY
27	SCARLET	RED	VENETIAN RED	BRIGHT RED RAYED AZURE
28	VIOLET	SKY BLUE	BLUEISH MAUVE	WHITE TINGED PURPLE
29	CRIMSON (ULTRA VIOLET)	BUFF, FLECKED SILVER-WHITE	LIGHT TRANSLUCENT BROWN	STONE COLOUR
30	ORANGE	GOLD YELLOW	RICH AMBER	AMBER RAYED RED
31	GLOWING ORANGE SCARLET	VERMILLION	SCARLET, FLECKED GOLD	VERMILLION FLECKED CRIMSON & EMERALD
32	INDIGO	BLACK	BLUE BLACK	BLACK RAYED BLUE
32 BIS	CITRINE+RUSSET+OLIVE+BLACK	AMBER	DARK BROWN	BLACK AND YELLOW
31 BIS	WHITE, MERGING GREY	DEEP PURPLE	THE 7 PRISMATIC COLOURS, THE VIOLET BEING OUTSIDE	WHITE, RED, YELLOW, BLUE, BLACK

KEY SCALE	XI EGYPTIAN DEITIES	XII HINDU DEITIES	XIII NORSE DEITIES
0	HARPOCRATES, AMOUN, NUIT	AUM	
1	PTAH, ASAR UN NEFER, HERU-RA-HA, HADIT	PARABRAHM	WOTAN
2	TAHUTI, AMOUN, NUIT (ZODIAC)	SHIVA, VISHNU, AKASA, LINGAM	ODIN
3	MAUT, ISIS, NEPHTYS	BHAVANI (ALL FORMS OF SAKTI), PRANA, YONI	FRIGGA
4	AMOUN, ISIS (HATHOOR)	INDRA, BRAHMA	WOTAN
5	HORUS, NEPHTYS	VISHNU, VARRUNA-AVATAR	THOR
6	ASAR, RA (ON, HRUMACHIS)	VISHU-HARI-KRISHNA-RAMA	
7	HATHOOR	BHAVANI	FREYA
8	ANUBIS	HANUMAN	ODIN, LOKI
9	SHU, HERMANUBIS, ALL PHALLIC GODS	GANESHA, VISHNU (KURM AVATAR)	
10	SEB, LOWER ISIS AND NEPHTYS, SPHINX	LAKSHIMI, KUNDALINI	
11	NU (HOOR-PA-KRAAT AS ATU 0)	THE MARUTS (VAYU)	VALKYRIES
12	TAHUTI AND CYNOCEPHALUS	HANUMAN, VISHNU (AS PARASA-RAMA)	
13	CHOMSE	CHANDRA AS 🌙	
14	HATHOR	LALITA (SEXUAL ASPECT OF SAKTI)	FREYA
15	MEN THU	SHIVA	
16	ASAR, AMESHET, APIS	SHIVA (SACRED BULL)	
17	TWIN DEITIES, REKHT, MERTI	VARIOUS TWIN AND HYBRID DEITIES	
18	KHEPRA	KRISHNA	
19	RA-HOOR-KHUIT, PASHT, SEKHET, MAU	VISHNU (NARA-SINGH-AVATAR)	
20	ISIS AS VIRGIN	THE GOPI GIRLS, LORD OF YOGA	
21	AMOUN RA	BRAHMA, INDRA	
22	MA	YAMA	
23	TUM, PTAH, AURAMOTH AS ▽, ASAR AS HANGED MAN	SOMA	
24	MERTI GODDESSES, TYPHON, APEP	KUNDALINI	
25	NEPHTYS	VISHNU (HORSE-AVATAR)	
26	KHEM (SET)	LINGAM, YONI	
27	HORUS	KRISHNA	
28	AHEPI , ARQUERIS	THE MARUTS	TUISCO
29	KHEPRA AS SCARAB IN TAROT TRUMP	VISHNU (MATSYA-AVATAR)	
30	RA AND MANY OTHERS	AGNI (TEJAS) YAMA (GOD OF LAST JUDGEMENT)	
31	THOUM-AESH-NEITH, MAU, KABESHUNT, TARPESHETH	SURYA AS ☉	
32	SEBEK, MAKO	BRAHMA	
32 BIS	SATEM, AHAPSI, NEPHTYS, AMESHET	PRITHIVI	
31 BIS	ASAR	AKASA	

KEY SCALE	XIV GREEK DEITIES	XV ROMAN DEITIES	XVI CHRISTIAN EGREGORES
0	PAN		
1	ZEUS, IACCHUS	JUPITER	GOD THE 3 IN 1
2	ATHENA, URANUS (HERMES)	JANUS (MERCURY)	GOD THE FATHER
3	CYBELE, DEMETER, RHEA, HERE, PSYCHE, KRONOS	JUNO, CYBELE, HECATE	THE VIRGIN MARY
4	POSEIDON (ZEUS)	JUPITER (LIBITINA)	GOD THE RAIN-MAKER
5	ARES, HADES	MARS	CHRIST COMING TO JUDGE THE WORLD
6	IACCHUS, APOLLO, ADONIS, DIONYSUS, BACCHUS	APOLLO (BACCHUS, AURORA)	GOD THE SON
7	APHRODITE, NIKE	VENUS	MESSIAH, LORD OF HOSTS
8	HERMES	MERCURY	GOD THE HOLY GHOST/HEALER OF PLAGUES
9	ZEUS AS △, DIANA OF EPHESUS AS PHALLIC STONE AND ⌣, EROS	DIANA AS ⌣ (TERMINUS JUPITER)	GOD THE HOLY GHOST (AS INCUBUS)
10	PERSEPHONE, ADONIS, PSYCHE	CERES	ECCLESIA XSTI, THE VIRGIN MARY
11	ZEUS	JUPITER (JUNO, EOLUS)	MATTHEW
12	HERMES	MERCURY	SARDIS
13	ARTEMIS, HEKATE	DIANA	LAODICEA
14	APHRODITE	VENUS	THYATIRA
15	ATHENA	MARS, MINERVA	(THE DISCIPLES ARE TOO INDEFINITE)
16	HERE	VENUS	
17	CASTOR AND POLLUX, APOLLO THE DIVINER, EROS	CASTOR AND POLLUX, (JANUS)	
18	APOLLO THE CHARIOTEER	MERCURY (LARES AND PENATES)	
19	DEMETER (BORNE BY LIONS)	VENUS (REPRESSING THE FIRES OF VULCAN)	
20	ATTIS	ATTIS	
21	ZEUS	JUPITER (PLUTO)	PHILADELPHIA
22	THEMIS, MINOS, AEACUS, RHADAMANTHUS	VULCAN (VENUS, NEMESIS)	
23	POSEIDON	NEPTUNE (RHEA)	JOHN, JESUS AS HANGED MAN
24	ARES (APOLLO THE PYTHEAN, THANATOS)	MARS (MORS)	
25	APOLLO, ARTEMIS (HUNTERS)	DIANA AS ARCHER (IRIS)	
26	PAN, PRIAPUS (ERECT HERMES AND BACCHUS)	PAN, VESTA, BACCHUS	
27	ARES (ATHENA)	MARS	PERGAMON
28	ATHENA, GANYMEDE	JUNO (AEOLUS)	
29	POSEIDON (HERMES PSYCHOPOMPOS)	NEPTUNE	
30	HELIOS, APOLLO	APOLLO (OPS)	SMYRNA
31	HADES	VULCAN, PLUTO	MARK
32	ATHENA	SATURN (TERMINUS ASTRAEA)	EPHESUS
32 BIS	DEMETER, GAIA	CERES	LUKE
31 BIS	IACCHUS	(LIBER) (BACCHUS)	THE HOLY GHOST

KEY SCALE	XVII MAGICAL WEAPONS	XVIII MAGICAL FORMULA	XIX MAGICAL POWERS
0	NO ATTRIBUTION POSSIBLE	LASTAL, M....M	SUPREME ATTAINMENT, VISION OF NO DIFFERENCE
1	SWASTIKA OR FYLFOT CROSS, CROWN, (THE LAMP)		UNION WITH GOD
2	LINGAM, THE INNER ROBE OF GLORY (THE WORD)	VIAOV	VISION OF GOD FACE TO FACE (VISION OF ANTINOMIES)
3	YONI, THE OUTER ROBE OF CONCEALMENT (THE CUP, THE SHINING STAR)	BABALON, VITRIOL	VISION OF SORROW, VISION OF WONDER
4	THE WAND, CENTRE OR CROOK	IHVH	VISION OF LOVE
5	THE SWORD, SPEAR, SCOURGE, CHAIN	AGLA, ALHIM, ABRAHADABRA	VISION OF POWER
6	THE LAMEN OR ROSY CROSS	IAO: INRI	VISION OF THE HARMONY OF THINGS, MYSTERIES OF CRUCIFIXION
7	THE LAMP AND GIRDLE	ARARITA	THE VISION OF BEAUTY TRIUMPHANT
8	THE NAMES AND VERSICLES AND APRON		THE VISION OF SPLENDOUR (EZEKIEL)
9	THE PERFUMES AND SANDALS	ALIM	THE VISION OF THE MACHINERY OF THE UNIVERSE
10	THE MAGICAL CIRCLE AND TRIANGLE	VITRIOL	THE VISION OF THE HOLY GUARDIAN ANGEL OR OF ADONAI
11	THE DAGGER OR FAN		DIVINATION
12	THE WAND OR CADUCEUS		MIRACLES OF HEALING, GIFT OF TONGUES, KNOWLEDGE OF SCIENCES
13	BOW AND ARROW	ALIM	THE WHITE TINCTURE, CLAIRVOYANCE, DIVINATION BY DREAMS
14	THE GIRDLE	AGAPE	LOVE-PHILTRES
15	THE HORNS, ENERGY, THE BURIN		POWER OF CONSECRATING THINGS
16	THE LABOUR OF PREPARATION (THRONE AND ALTAR)		THE SECRET OF PHYSICAL STRENGTH
17	THE TRIPOD		POWER OF BEING IN TWO PLACES AT ONE TIME, PROPHECY
18	THE FURNACE (CUP OR HOLY GRAIL)	ABRAHADABRA	POWER OF CASTING ENCHANTMENTS
19	THE DISCIPLE (PRELIMINARY) (PHOENIX WAND)	TO MEGA THERION	POWER OF TRAINING WILD BEASTS
20	THE LAMP AND THE WAND, THE BREAD (LOTUS WAND)		INVISIBILITY, PARTHENOGENESIS INITIATION
21	THE SCEPTRE		ACQUIRING POLITICAL AND OTHER ASCENDENCY
22	THE CROSS OF EQUILIBRIUM		WORKS OF JUSTICE AND EQUILIBRIUM
23	THE CUP AND CROSS OF SUFFERING, THE WINE (WATER OF LUSTRATION)		THE GREAT WORK, TALISMANS, CRYSTAL GAZING
24	THE PAIN OF OBLIGATION (THE OATH)	AUMGN	NECROMANCY
25	THE ARROW (SWIFT AND STRAIGHT APPLICATION OF FORCE)	ON	TRANSMUTATIONS, VISION OF THE UNIVERSAL PEACOCK
26	THE SECRET FORCE, LAMP	ON	THE WITCHES' SABBATH SO CALLED, THE EVIL EYE
27	THE SWORD		WORKS OF WRATH AND VENGEANCE
28	THE CENSER OR ASPERGILLUS		ASTROLOGY
29	THE TWILIGHT OF THE PLACE AND MAGIC MIRROR	IAO: INRI	BEWITCHMENTS, CASTING ILLUSIONS
30	THE LAMEN OR BOW AND ARROW		THE RED TINCTURE, POWER OF ACQUIRING WEALTH
31	THE WAND, THE LAMP, THE THURIBLE		EVOCATION, PYROMANCY
32	A SICKLE		WORKS OF MALE DICTION AND DEATH
32 BIS	THE PENTACLE OR BREAD AND SALT		ALCHEMY, GEOMANCY, MAKING PENTACLES, ASTRAL TRAVEL
31 BIS	THE WINGED EGG		INVISIBILITY, TRANSFORMATIONS, VISION OF THE GENIUS

KEY SCALE	XX ANIMALS REAL AND IMAGINARY	XXI PLANTS REAL AND IMAGINARY	XXII PRECIOUS STONES
0	DRAGON	LOTUS, ROSE	STAR SAPPHIRE, BLACK DIAMOND
1	GOD (SWAN, HAWK)	ALMOND IN FLOWER, BANYAN	DIAMOND
2	MAN	AMARANTH, MISTLETOE, BO OR PIPAL	STAR RUBY, TURQUOISE
3	WOMAN (BEE)	CYPRESS, OPIUM POPPY, LOTUS, LILY, IVY	STAR SAPPHIRE, PEARL
4	UNICORN	OLIVE, SHAMROCK, OPIUM POPPY	AMETHYST, SAPPHIRE, LAPIS LAZULI
5	BASILISK	OAK, NUR VOMICA, NETTLE, HICKORY	RUBY
6	PHOENIX, LION, CHILD, SPIDER, PELICAN	ACACIA, BAY, LAUREL, VINE, OAK, ASH, GORSE	TOPAZ, YELLOW DIAMOND
7	LYNX, RAVEN,	ROSE, LAUREL	EMERALD
8	HERMAPHRODITE, JACKAL, TWIN SERPENTS	MOLY, ANHALONIUM LEWINII	OPAL, FIRE OPAL
9	ELEPHANT, TORTOISE, TOAD	BANYAN, MANDRAKE, DAMIANA, GINSENG	QUARTZ
10	SPHINX	WILLOW, LILY, POMEGRANATE, ALL CEREALS	ROCK CRYSTAL
11	EAGLE, MAN, CHERUB OF △, OX	ASPEN	TOPAZ
12	SWALLOW, IBIS, APE, TWIN SERPENTS, FISH-HYBRIDS	VERVAIN, HERB MERCURY, PALM, LIME, LINDEN	OPAL, AGATE
13	DOG, STORK, CAMEL	ALMOND, MUGWORT, HAZEL, MOONWORT	MOONSTONE, PEARL, CRYSTAL
14	SPARROW, DOVE, SWAN, SOW, ALL BIRDS	MYRTLE, ROSE, CLOVER, PEACH, APPLE	EMERALD, TURQUOISE
15	RAM, OWL	TIGER LILY, GERANIUM, OLIVE	RUBY
16	BULL (CHERUB OF ▽), ALL BEASTS OF BURDEN	MALLOW, ALL GIANT TREES	TOPAZ
17	MAGPIE, HYBRIDS, PARROTS, ZEBRA, PENGUIN	HYBRIDS, ORCHIDS	ALEXANDRITE, TOURMALINE
18	CRAB, TURTLE, SPHINX, WHALE	LOTUS	AMBER
19	LION (CHERUB OF △), CAT, TIGER, SERPENT, WOMAN)	SUNFLOWER	CAT'S EYE
20	VIRGIN, ANCHORITE, RHINOCEROS	SNOWDROP, LILY, NARCISSUS, MISTLETOE	PERIDOT
21	EAGLE, PRAYING MANTIS	HYSSOP, OAK, POPULAR, FIG, ARNICA, CEDAR	AMETHYST, LAPIS LAZULI
22	ELEPHANT, SPIDER	ALOE	EMERALD
23	EAGLE-SNAKE-SCORPION (CHERUB OF▽)	LOTUS, ALL WATER PLANTS	BERYL, AQUAMARINE
24	SCORPION, BEETLE, CRAYFISH, WOLF	CACTUS, NETTLE, ALL POISONOUS PLANTS	SNAKESTONE, GREENISH TURQUOISE
25	CENTAUR, HORSE, HIPPOGRIFF, DOG	RUSH	JACINTH
26	GOAT, ASS, OYSTER	INDIAN HEMP, ORCHIS ROOT, THISTLE	BLACK DIAMOND
27	HORSE, BEAR, WOLF, BOAR	ABSINTHE, RUE	RUBY, ALL RED STONES
28	MAN OR EAGLE (CHERUB OF△), PEACOCK	OLIVE, COCONUT	ARTIFICIAL GLASS
29	FISH, DOLPHIN, BEETLE, DOG, JACKAL	UNICELLULAR ORGANISMS, OPIUM	PEARL
30	LION, SPARROWHAWK, LEOPARD	SUNFLOWER, LAURAL, HELIOTROP, GALANGAL	CRYSOLITH
31	LION (CHERUB OF△)	RED POPPY, HIBISCUS, ALL SCARLET FLOWERS	FIRE OPAL
32	CROCODILE	ASH, CYPRESS, HELLEBORE, YEW, NIGHTSHADE	ONYX
32 BIS	BULL (CHERUB OF▽)	OAK, IVY, CEREALS	SALT
31 BIS	SPHINX (IF SWORDED OR CROWNED)	ALMOND IN FLOWER	BLACK DIAMOND

KEY SCALE	XXIII PERFUMES	XXIV VEGETABLE DRUGS	XXV MINERAL DRUGS
0	NO ATTRIBUTION POSSIBLE		
1	AMBERGRIS	ELIXIR VITAE	CARBON
2	MUSK	HASHISH, COCAINE	AUR, POT
3	MYRRH, CIVET	BELLADONNA, SOMA	PHOSPHORUS
4	CEDAR	OPIUM	SILVER
5	TOBACCO	NUN VOMICA, NETTLE, COCAINE, ATROPINE	
6	OLIBANUM	STRAMONIUM, ALCOHOL, DIGITALIS, COFFEE	IRON, SULPHUR
7	BENZOIN, ROSE, RED SANDAL	DAMIANA, CANNABIS INDICA, ANHALONIUM	
8	STORAX	ANHALONIUM LEWINII, CANNABIS INDICA	ARSENIC
9	JASMINE, JINSENG	ORCHID ROOT	MERCURY
10	DITTANY OF CRETE	CORN	LEAD
11	GALBANUM	PEPPERMINT	MAG, SULPH
12	MASTIC, WHITE SANDAL, MACE, STORAX	ALL CEREBRAL EXCITANTS	
13	MENSTRUAL BLOOD, CAMPHOR, ALOES	JUPITER, PENNYROYAL	MERCURY
14	SANDALWOOD, MYRTLE	ALL APHRODISIACS	
15	DRAGON'S BLOOD	ALL CEREBRAL EXCITANTS	
16	STORAX	SUGAR	
17	WORMWOOD	ERGOT AND ECBOLICS	
18	ONYCHA	WATERCRESS	
19	OLIBANUM	ALL CARMINATIVES AND TONICS	
20	NARCISSUS	ALL ANAPHRODISIACS	
21	SAFFRON	COCAINE	
22	GALBANUM	TOBACCO	
23	ONYCHA, MYRRH	CASEARA, ALL PURGES	SULPHATES
24	SIAMESE BENZOIN, OPOPONAX		
25	LIGN-ALOES		
26	MUSK, CIVET, SATURNIAN PERFUMES	ORCHIS, SATYRION	
27	PEPPER, DRAGON'S BLOOD		
28	GALBANUM	ALL DIURETICS	
29	AMBERGRIS, MENSTRUAL FLUID	ALL NARCOTICS	
30	OLIBANUM, CINNAMON	ALCOHOL	
31	OLIBANUM, FIERY ODOURS		NITRATES
32	ASAFOETIDA, SCAMMONY, SULPHUR, INDIGO		LEAD
32 BIS	STORAX, ALL DULL AND HEAVY ODOURS		BISMUTH
31 BIS	NO ATTRIBUTION POSSIBLE	STRAMONIUM	CARBON

KEY SCALE	XXVI LETTERS OF THE NAME	XXVII ELEMENTS AND SENSES		XXVIII ARCHANGELS OF THE QUARTERS	
11	י	△	AIR, SMELL	רפאל	RAPHAEL
23	ה	▽	WATER, TASTE	גבריאל	GABRIEL
31	ו	△	FIRE, SIGHT	מיכאל	MICHAEL
32 BIS	ה	▽	EARTH, TOUCH	אוריאל	AURIEL
32 BIS	ש	⊛	SPIRIT, HEARING		

KEY SCALE	XXIX THE FOUR WORLDS		XXX PARTS OF THE SOUL		XXXI THE BODY
11	יצירה	YETZIRAH, FORMATIVE WORLD	רוח	RUACH	BREATH
23	בריאה	BRIAH, CREATIVE WORLD	נשמה	NESHAMAH	CHYLE, LYMPH
31	אצילות	ATZILUTH, ARCHETYPAL WORLD	חיה	CHIAH	BLOOD
32 BIS	עשיה	ASSIAH, MATERIAL WORLD	נפש	NEPHESH	SOLID STRUCTURES, TISSUES
32 BIS			יהידה	YECHIDAH	SEMEN, MARROW

All of that might seem like a LOT of information to take in. But, consider that, traditionally, the student was tasked with memorizing all of those (and more!) from the get-go. So, instead, I am asking you to start looking at them a little bit daily so that they might begin seeding inside your subconscious.

If we take an example, the use of the table will become clear.

Let us suppose that you wish to obtain knowledge of some obscure sciences – such as magick. You can construct a ritual with that aim in mind using correspondences.

Check out our Table above. Go to Column XIX, line 12, and you will find *Knowledge of Sciences.*

By looking up line 12 in the other columns, you will find that the corresponding planet is Mercury, and its number eight. The god who rules that planet is Thoth, or in Hebrew symbolism Tetragrammaton Adonai and Elohim Tzabaotz. Its colours are orange (for Mercury is the sphere of the eighth sephirah, Hod), yellow, purple, grey, and indigo rayed with violet. Its magical weapon is the wand or caduceus, its perfumes mastic and others, its sacred plants vervain and others, its jewel the opal or agate; its sacred animal the snake, and so on.

In magick, if we wish to master one particular idea, we must ensure that every component of the ritual we are attempting directly suggests that idea.

Thus in the ritual here, if your glance falls upon the orange lights you set up in the room, their colour will suggest Mercury; if you smell the perfumes, again, Mercury is brought to his mind. In fact, the whole exercise is nothing but a complex system of mnemonics.

All clear so far?

A NOTE ON CULTURAL APPROPRIATION

As I mentioned above, the Hermetic Qabalah we will make great use of derives directly from Christian Qabalah first and, more importantly, from Jewish Kabbalah.

Aleister Crowley, and his contemporaries, didn't see any inherent problem in taking ideas left and right from all the different cultures they came in touch with. But, nowadays, we must admit that a big part of this approach was fuelled by the staunch imperialism and colonialism at the backbone of these people's culture. Therefore, the discourse around cultural appropriation is fundamental because, as a society, we are finally discussing complex topics. Adopting cultural elements of a minority group in an exploitative, disrespectful, or stereotypical way is not ok any more – and it never was.

At the same time, I would also argue that it's essential to strike a balance just right and accept that religion, spirituality, mysticism, and magick have grown throughout history through accretion and syncretism.

A quick tour through occult Twitter or WitchTok will show you how the discourse on cultural appropriation has become wholly polarized, with wild takes on both sides. My suggestion is to always be respectful of the sources and, when speaking about Qabalah (with a Q), make it clear that it's a very different practice than its ancestor.

TAROT AS PORTAL

Pathworking is a Qabalistic concept that is similar to the process of a journey. It is a voyage into your inner self.

Pathworking with tarot helps you draw from the chosen card's energy, thereby assisting you in performing specific actions to achieve the desired outcome. For example, pathworking with the Eight of Disks can help improve your work ethic. Likewise, doing it with The Fool will help you gather the impetus to move on to a new adventure in your life. You get the gist.

Before attempting it, one should be acquainted with the meaning of the tarot cards and their place on the Tree of Life. A perfect opportunity to double down the study of the correspondences!

When used in connection with the tarot, pathworking becomes a process of entering a tarot card and interacting with the symbols and the characters within it – effectively using the tarot as a portal.

The idea is to step into the scenery of a particular card and explore it deeply. This technique is a powerful way to visualize your goals and plot your course – from where you are to where you want to be. It is a method that allows you to actively interact with the universe and co-create your life.

Pathworking also helps you to develop a deeper and more personal understanding of the cards and their meanings and interpretations. This, in turn, makes it easy to draw from the card's energy to assist in manifesting desired outcomes.

THE PROCESS

1. Sit or lie down comfortably. If you tend to fall asleep quickly, choose to sit down. Doing this exercise at least an hour after a meal is best to avoid falling asleep during the process. Moreover, it may also hamper your vision. At the same time, being hungry can also be a distraction, so avoid working on an

empty stomach. Having a snack after the pathworking process will help to ground you.

2. Use the bathroom before you begin. Wear comfortable, loose-fitting clothes. Take off your shoes. Most importantly, put aside all worries and mental distractions. Keep writing materials handy to note down your experiences and messages if you receive any.

3. Place your chosen card in front of you. It might be helpful to give more gravitas to the experience by lighting a candle and burning incense, both chosen according to the proper correspondences related to the card you want to enter.

4. With your eyes closed, start breathing more intensely. So inhale for four seconds, hold for two, exhale for four seconds, and finally hold again for two.

5. Project yourself mentally into the backdrop of the card and imbibe everything that it has to offer.

   a.   Here's a specific example, using the traditional imagery for the Four of Disks card to attract financial stability and material gain. Please note that I am using the imagery from Crowley & Harris *Thoth Tarot*.

   b.   Begin by focusing your attention on the card.

   c.   Close your eyes, and visualize yourself walking toward this magnificent castle. Its walls are made of pure gold, and its inhabitants celebrate the arrival of someone important: you.

   d.   As you cross the moat and enter the inner courtyard, a fanfare of trumpets resounds loudly, and everyone erupts in applause.

   e.   You are led to a catafalque assembled in the centre and offered the seat of honour on it. There you are presented with a chest of pure platinum: you open it and find it full to the brim of gold coins, precious gems, and jewels.

f. Take all the time you need to stuff your pockets with these riches and bask in the glory you are receiving.

6. Relax and allow your breath to return to normal, imbibing the card's energy.

7. Note your experiences and insights in a diary or journal for further reference (a little further on, we will discuss the practice of the magical diary).

As always, this will feel difficult at first as you are trying to juggle many different things at once: the breathing, the internal visualization, the thoughts, feelings, and emotions arising from the whole process, and finally – and most importantly – the potential messages coming from the card itself.

Maybe add one card a week to your daily practice in the coming weeks. For example, you could start with the Major Arcana and follow the Journey of the Fool, or as mentioned above, with specific cards trying to conjure particular results.

DAILY PRACTICE (DURATION: 1 WEEK)

Time for your first homework, and it's a straightforward one. Study the correspondence table for the next week. Make a copy of this image of an empty Tree of Life:

Then do the following:

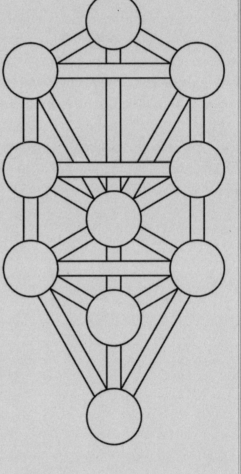

1. Assign the name of each sephiroth correctly.

2. Once you have done it, move on to the 22 paths that connect each sephiroth.

3. Assign a Hebrew letter and then a tarot Major Arcana card to each path.

4. Start using the tarot as a portal, with one card per week. There are 78 of them, so be ready for a long journey!

With just the right amount of theory behind you, it's time to move to something more practical.

THE FOUNDATIONS OF THE MAGICAL PYRAMID

CHAPTER 2

THE FOUNDATIONS OF THE MAGICAL PYRAMID

This is the start of our journey toward Heliopolis, the City of the Sun and the cradle of initiation. To reach it, we must travel upwards and build a mystical temple inside ourselves. We can call it a magical pyramid, and we are laying its foundations with these lessons.

Some of the lessons in this chapter will be incredibly boring for some of you. I will not pretend it's not if you already have a background in meditation and yoga. Still, without these strong foundations, we cannot hope to reach our goal. So stick with them, and you will move on to something that feels more magical in no time.

BREATHE. NOW. ALWAYS. CONSCIOUSLY.

For the coming month, I would like each of you to set aside 10 minutes a day where you turn off the phone, the computer, the TV, and even music (we will bring this one back on at some point) and focus on these simple points:

- Sit comfortably, spine erect, shoulders relaxed. If you can't sit, laying on the floor is OK, as long as the spine is straight.

- Close your eyes
- Learn to breathe

By learning to breathe, I mean it: pay close attention to your breathing pattern and immediately realize how often we pay no attention to it. Most of our days are spent without ever giving breathing any attention whatsoever, and we end up holding it to our detriment. Maybe you are doing it right now, as you are reading these words. Make the conscious effort to remember to breathe, always:

- When you walk or drive to work
- When you speak with others
- When you are watching Netflix

One 'magical' word for breathing is *prana*, from the Sanskrit: it means more than breath, as it can also be used to convey the idea of energy. Thus learning to control breathing is *pranayama*, one of the eight limbs of yoga.

I will not mince words here: **if you can't breathe or control this precise kind of energy, there is no magick**. No matter how many extraordinary wordy rituals you commit to memory or how many magical tools you make or buy, if there's no breathing, there's no magick. If anyone tells you differently, they are either clueless or lying. So to clarify: there are numerous breathing techniques, but the above is sufficient for now.

ALLOW FOR THOUGHTS, EMOTIONS, FEELINGS, AND BODY SENSATIONS TO ARISE

Moving on from that hot take, the next step is to allow for thoughts, passions, feelings and body sensations. Then, using a more magical vocabulary, you must learn to become acquainted with the **hermetic elements** of **Air** (thoughts), **Fire** (passions and the creative impulses), **Water** (feelings and emotions), and **Earth** (body sensations). This will establish your own magical circle, your own magical temple – that is, your **body of light**, which is also the magical circle. By that, I mean that while specific techniques, especially Solomonic conjurations, require the magician to draw an actual circle around themselves to signify their established authority over the universe, these external props represent the magician's own mastery of *prana* itself. They are undoubtedly helpful and definitely very picturesque at first. But with years of practice and progress, you won't need them any more. Disclaimer: this book's exercises will only get you started!

Without a strong body of light, you will not be able to get in touch with spirits, gods, angels, demons, and all the plethora of ultraterrestrials across the planes of existence. And since I bet that's what you want to do, better start building that body of light.

When you allow your thoughts or emotions to surface, you should never lose yourself in them. If a memory arises while you are in a meditative state, allow yourself to experience it without letting it become the proper focus of the practice.

LEARN TO VISUALIZE: THE CREATION OF REAL OR UNREAL IMAGES IN THE MIND'S EYE

People tend to find this either very easy or very difficult. This is not meant to be a judgement in any way. Some people are audio learners, some find writing easy, and some naturally have a more visual imagination. Still, it's a skill that can be learned by all. Here's a secret for those who find it difficult: visualization means the conscious act of wanting to create an image in the mind. Keep doing it, and eventually, you will succeed.

THE FOUR HERMETIC ELEMENTS

As it developed in Europe between the 10th and 17th centuries, Western esotericism was based mainly on traditional astrology. We owe most of the groundwork to Agrippa's monumental opus, *Three Books of Occult Philosophy*.[6]

The tropical zodiac's directional correspondences are taken from the solstices and equinoxes as seen from the northern hemisphere. The sun reaches its highest northern latitude during the summer solstice (Cancer), and its southernmost latitude during the winter solstice (Capricorn). We can map the other cardinal directions using these cardinal points:

- Aries – East
- Cancer – North
- Libra – West
- Capricorn – South

In addition, each of the 12 signs is allocated an element in the following order: Fire, Earth, Air, and Water. When you examine the elements by their fundamental properties, the reasoning behind this becomes clear. Due to the rigorous dualistic mindset of the time, Agrippa also ascribed gender to them:

- Fire – masculine, hot and dry
- Earth – feminine, cold and dry
- Air – masculine, hot and moist
- Water – feminine, cold and moist

---

[6] Heinrich Cornelius Agrippa von Nettesheim (14 September 1486–18 February 1535) was a German polymath, physician, legal scholar, soldier, theologian, and occult writer. Agrippa's *Three Books of Occult Philosophy* published in 1533 drew heavily upon Kabbalah, hermeticism, and neo-Platonism. His book was widely influential among occultists of the early modern period, and was condemned as heretical by the inquisitor of Cologne. (*Wikipedia*)

While each element can be turned into any other element, it usually transforms into another element that shares one of its basic characteristics. Fire, for example, can more easily transform into Air (because it is also hot) or Earth (because it is also dry) than it can into Water. The zodiac's order of the elements is the only method to keep both patterns.

The elements also correlate to the modalities in a predetermined manner. For example, the first sign of a season is cardinal, followed by fixed and mutable.[7] The cardinal elements correspond to the four compass points, as seen below:

Sign	Direction	Element
Aries	East	Cardinal Fire
Taurus	East of northeast	Fixed Earth
Gemini	North of northeast	Mutable Air
Cancer	North	Cardinal Water
Leo	North of northwest	Fixed Fire
Virgo	West of northwest	Mutable Earth
Libra	West	Cardinal Air
Scorpio	West of southwest	Fixed Water
Sagittarius	South of southwest	Mutable Fire
Capricorn	South	Cardinal Earth
Aquarius	South of southeast	Fixed Air
Pisces	East of southeast	Mutable Water

Above: The zodiac with the compass directions
and the relative elements

---

[7] Cardinal signs, fixed signs, and mutable signs are the three modalities in astrology (sometimes known as quadruplicities because each group has four zodiac signs). These classifications describe the distinct ways in which each sign shows their energy, reacts to various circumstances, and functions in the world as they progress through life.

When Éliphas Lévi[8] and the Hermetic Order of the Golden Dawn set up to revitalize the magical current, they took Agrippa's structure and reasoning. Then, they created the hexagram ritual to represent the macrocosmic perspective (literally, looking at the Heavens). You will get here by reaching the pinnacle of this magical pyramid you are starting to build.

Once they had done that, they reasoned they would need a different ritual to represent the microcosmic perspective and how the elements interacted upon Earth instead of how they do it in the Heavens. So this is how the pentagram rituals came to be. By practising them, you will find a different progression of the elements since the progression follows the path of the sun in Earth's skies from dawn to dusk and into the night.

Station of the sun	Direction	Element
Dawn	East	Air
Noon	South	Fire
Sunset	West	Water
Midnight	North	Earth

Above: The stations of the sun with the compass directions and the relative elements

Bottom line: these are only maps. You can find a reason for them, but for me, it's more critical *to do the ritual itself* until it's mastered and its lessons are integrated. In the case of the pentagram: recognition and refinement of the elemental energies in our immediate surroundings and on this plane.

---

[8] Éliphas Lévi Zahed, born Alphonse Louis Constant (8 February 1810–31 May 1875), was a French esotericist, poet, and author of more than 20 books on magic, Kabbalah, alchemical studies, and occultism. He pursued an ecclesiastical career in the Catholic Church until, after great personal struggle, at the age of 26, he abandoned the Roman Catholic priesthood. At the age of 40, he began professing knowledge of the occult, and becoming a reputed ceremonial magician. (*Wikipedia*)

For the hexagram: how these elemental energies mutate when reflected on the Heavens, when they begin to interact and merge with the planetary influences.

THE MAGICAL DIARY

The last step for this first lesson is to acquire a (magical) diary and write a short report after each practice session.

Aleister Crowley insisted that all experiments must be recorded in detail during or after their performance. Therefore, take notice of your physical and mental condition. It's also essential to record the time and the place and what kind of weather it was outside. If you are already into astrology, record that data as well: the position of the sun and the moon in the zodiac, if Mercury is retrograde, and so on. Finally, you must aim to record all conditions that might have influenced the practice: either positive or negative.

One key point is not to spend too much time pontificating in your head what the final end of these practices might be. Instead, just do them, and record them. Another thing is to try and rely solely on your intelligence and not let other people's experiences and reports influence your practice.

However, this doesn't mean you shouldn't trust more experienced practitioners! Another thing Crowley insisted on is that this magical diary should be prepared so that others could benefit from its study. His own *John St John*, published in the first volume of *The Equinox*, is an example of this kind of record.

Finally, he clarified that the more *scientific* the record is, the better. Still, this is a magical record, after all. So you should never forget to always record your emotions as some of the conditions. This practice really is the key to scientific illuminism, one of the critical approaches of Thelema. The emphasis is on reproducibility. Rituals and exercises can be performed precisely so that they can be replicated by others. Likewise, you should get precise and reproducible results with practice: if not, the particular ritual or exercise you're doing is merely superstition.

Here follows an example of my own magical record. This one is relative to a group operation we ran in March 2021 ev. At the height of the lockdowns, we were running wild in the astral plane, looking for new clues about the nature of a potential ultraterrestrial consciousness known to us as TRW. And if this seems strange to you, consider that our starting point was a high strangeness TV show called *Hellier*. Magick IS weirder than you think! LAM, mentioned below, is the name of a preterhuman entity allegedly channelled by Crowley, according to his disciple Kenneth Grant. It has been heavily implied to be Crowley's artistic rendition of Aiwass himself (more on him later in the book). Surely it has inspired more than two generations and counting of magical pioneers with its enigmatic stare.

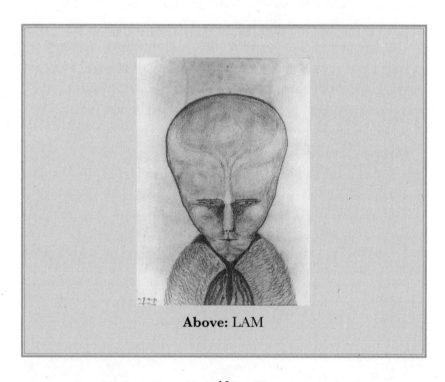

Above: LAM

Monday, 15 March 2021 ev – 11:15 pm GMT
Weather: wind WNW, foggy, 5° Celsius
Astrology: sun in Pisces, moon in Aries
Magick: LAM operation

As soon as I looked at the picture of LAM I felt pulled into it. I took it as a clear sign I was invited in, but I took nonetheless a little time before actually entering. This time, when closing my eyes, I didn't feel as dizzy as I have felt the previous times. My body felt like fast asleep: the body feeling physically heavy, while my mind felt floating inside. At one point I even felt like falling back on my pillow (I didn't – I kept sitting crossed-legged with my spine straight). My consciousness subdued. It is a very different environment than what I have been used to so far when meditating, or even after a Thelemic middle pillar. My field of vision was filled with fractals of all kinds of purple/mauve shades. I felt 'not alone' but could not see specific shapes. I 'call' to someone on my right and I see shockwaves rippling through the fractals. At one point I felt compelled to open my palms forward. Then, I heard a noise like a rapid frfrfrfrfrfr from behind my head (I really cannot compare it to anything I know) and started feeling extremely nauseous, so much so that I came out of it. As I opened my eyes, I took some time to regulate my breathing again, and to ground myself. Stood up, and closed the operation with a LBRP (Lesser Banishing Ritual of the Pentagram). Felt off for quite a while afterwards.

THE FOUR DAILY ADORATIONS

At the beginning of this chapter, I promised you that, soon enough, we would start engaging with practices that felt more magical. It's time to do so.

Since the dawn of time, humanity has worshipped the sun as the visible symbol of an unknown god that pervaded all creation. To declare our will to embark on this journey of spiritual evolution, we must reaffirm our connection to this source of life, love and liberty.

Aleister Crowley devised a ritual published as *Liber Resh vel Helios sub figurâ CC*,[9] composed of four adorations to be performed throughout the day. And while the unknown god we strive toward is unity, the sun (its symbol) appears differently at each of its four stations – dawn, noon, sunset, and midnight. Thus an adoration is directed toward the sun at each station.

So you will add these adorations to your daily practice. Of course, you can read them, but by the end of this first month, you should aim to have them committed to memory. This is because you are also called to visualize a specific god from the Egyptian pantheon and do a particular sign with your hands – see the images below.

---

[9]   I have attempted to streamline this ritual by modernizing its archaic tone. I have also simplified it a little bit, focusing solely on the invocations at the four stations of the sun. Purists will be likely to dissent here, and maybe that's not a bad thing.

DAWN (OR RIGHT AFTER WAKING UP)

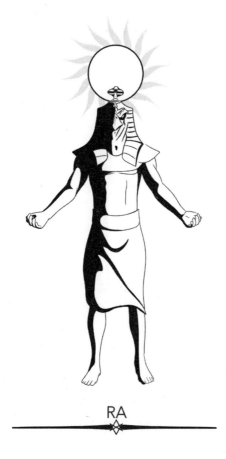

RA

Face east, and give the four signs depicted overleaf. Say in a loud voice:

Salutations to Ra in their rising and in their strength,
Who travels through the Heavens in their bark at dawn.
Tahuti, in his majesty, stands at the prow, and Ra-Hoor is at
the helm.
From the abodes of night, hails and salutations!

1

3

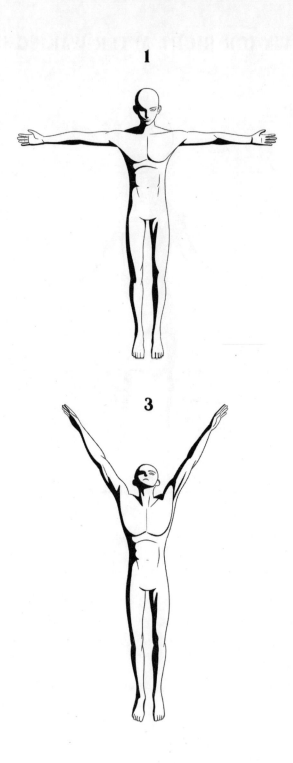

2

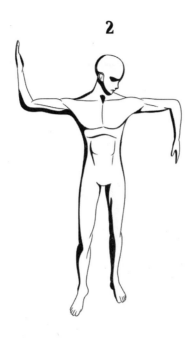

4

NOON

AHATHOOR

Face south, and give the sign depicted opposite. Say in a loud voice:

> Salutations to Ahathoor in their triumph and in their beauty,
> Who travels through the Heavens in their bark at the mid-
> course of the sun.
> Tahuti, in his majesty, stands at the prow, and Ra-Hoor is at
> the helm.
> From the abodes of morning, hails and salutations!

SIGN OF FIRE

THE GODDESS THOUM-AESH-NEITH

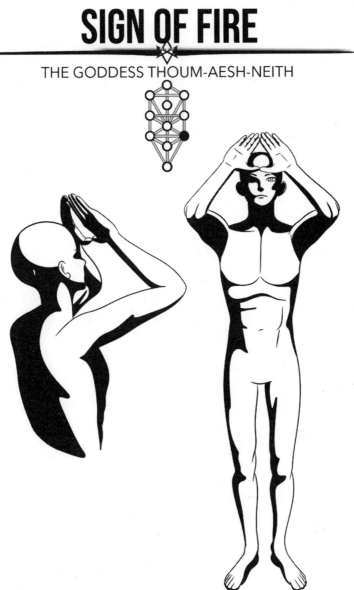

SUNSET

TUM

Face west, and give the sign depicted opposite. Say in a loud
voice:

> Salutations to Tum in their setting and in their joy,
> Who travels over the Heavens in their bark as the sun sets.
> Tahuti, in his majesty, stands at the prow, and Ra-Hoor is at
>   the helm.
> From the abodes of day, hails and salutations!

SIGN OF AIR

THE GOD SHU HOLDING THE SKY

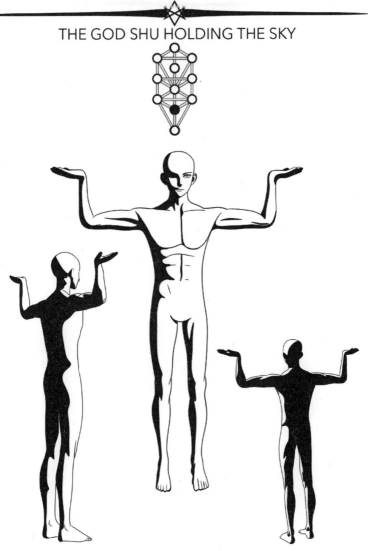

MIDNIGHT (OR BEFORE BEDTIME)

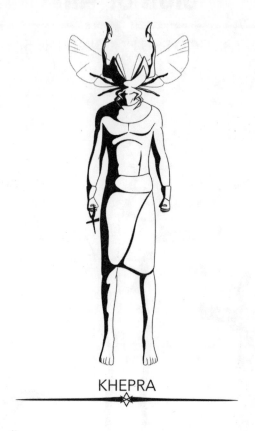

KHEPRA

Face north, and give the sign depicted opposite. Say in a loud voice:

Salutations to Khepra in their hiding and in their silence,
Who travels through the Heavens in their bark at the midnight
  hour of the sun.
Tahuti, in his majesty, stands at the prow, and Ra-Hoor is at
  the helm.
From the abodes of evening, hails and salutations!

SIGN OF WATER

THE GODDESS AURAMOTH

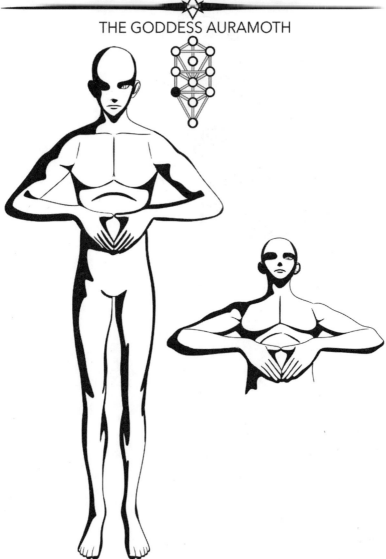

After each adoration, you should give the sign of silence.

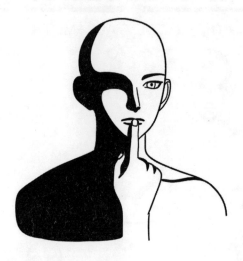

LIBER RESH VEL HELIOS

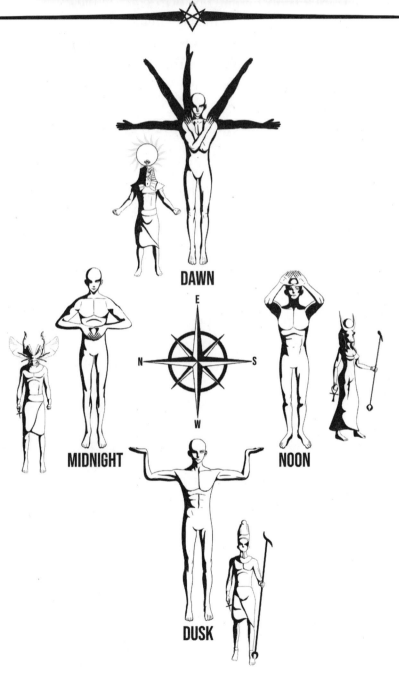

DAWN

MIDNIGHT

NOON

DUSK

Much of the symbolism hidden in this practice will be missed by you at this point. Why the Egyptian gods?[10] What are those signs we do? Do you really have to say these words out loud?

Grasping all the details at the beginning is impossible and detrimental to further progress. **Overthinking is the death of magick – I cannot emphasize this enough.** So let it not be an obstacle to your daily practice.

I would suggest from the start that it might be a good idea to apply yourself to it, **especially if you feel resistance toward doing it**.

This is the first practice that has a distinct quasi-religious feeling about it. That's precisely by design. If you are one of the many who feel somewhat repulsed by the idea of religion – as it's been shoved down our collective throats in the last 2,000 years of patriarchal abuse – then maybe confronting your prejudices about it will be twice as worthwhile.

To help you fight those resistances – if any arise – what follows might help you overcome them.

---

[10] It should be noted here that Crowley changed the Egyptian gods attributed to the stations of the sun here. Khepra is traditionally a god of dawn, not of midnight. Furthermore, the name Ahathoor really should be Hathor – but as we will notice later on, Crowley's grasp of Egyptian language wasn't the best. I suggest those interested in going deeper in traditional Egyptian magick see the books of Mogg Morgan of Mandrake, Oxford.

STEPPING OUT OF THE OLD AEON AND INTO THE NEW

Initially published in *The Equinox 3.1* in 1919, the article by Frater Achad,[11] 'Stepping out of the old aeon into the new', is the perfect companion to the practice and understanding of the practice we just introduced above.

It starts by stating that with the reception of *Liber AL vel Legis* in 1904, we have entered a new aeon. A higher truth has been given to the world. This truth is waiting in readiness for all who will consciously accept it, but it has to be realized before it is understood. Only then can one appreciate its beauty and perfection.

The new teaching appears strange at first. Furthermore, the mind cannot grasp more than a fragment of what it really means. Only when we live the law can that fragment expand into the infinite conception of the whole.

He continues saying that he wants to share one little fragment of this great truth, made clear to him on a Sunday (sun day, indeed) morning. So Achad asks you to go with him – if you will – just across the border-line of the old aeon and gaze for a moment at the new. He tells you that if your new perspective pleases you, then you can remain there. If not, you can quickly go back to where you come from. You will always be able to get there again, in the twinkling of an eye, just by readjusting your inner sight to the truth.

Humanity has always been deeply captivated by the ideas of sunrise and sunset. Our ancient brethren, seeing the sun

---

[11] Charles Robert Stansfeld Jones (1886–1950), aka Frater Achad, was an occultist and ceremonial magician. An early aspirant to the A∴A∴ (the 20th to be admitted as a Probationer, in December 1909) who 'claimed' the grade of Magister Templi as a neophyte. He also became an OTO initiate, serving as the principal organizer for that order in British Columbia, Canada. (*Wikipedia*)

disappear at night and rise again in the morning, based all their religious beliefs on this one conception of a dying and re-arisen god. This is the central idea of the religion of the old aeon, but we have left it behind us because although it seemed to be based on nature (and nature's symbols are always true), we learned it was only a mirage. Science eventually taught us it isn't the sun that rises and sets but the Earth on which we live, which revolves so that its shadow cuts us off from the sunlight during what we call night. The sun does not die, as the ancients thought; it is always shining, always radiating light and life. Take a moment to visualize the sun and how it shines in the early morning, midday, evening, and night. Have you thought about it thoroughly? You've crossed over from the old to the new aeon.

Let us now consider what has occurred. What did you do to conjure up this mental image of the eternal sun? You began by associating yourself with the sun. Then you stepped out of the consciousness of this planet; for a brief moment, you had to consider yourself a solar being. So why take another step back? You may have done so unintentionally because the light was so bright that it appeared to be darkness. But do it again, this time more thoroughly, and consider the implications for our understanding of the universe.

When we identify with the sun, we realize that we have become the source of light, that we, too, are now shining gloriously, but we also realize that the sunlight is no longer for us because we can no longer see the sun, any more than we could see ourselves in our little old-aeon consciousness.

The night is all around us, but it is the starlight of our lady Nuit's body where we live, move, and have our being. So, from this height, we look back on the small planet Earth, where we were a moment ago, and imagine ourselves as shedding our light on all those little individuals we have called our brothers and sisters, the slaves who serve.

However, we do not stop there. Consider the sun focusing his rays on one tiny spot, Earth, for a brief moment. So, what happens? It is burned, consumed, and then vanishes. But truth exists in our solar consciousness, and while we may glance for a moment at the little sphere we have left behind us, it is no longer there. There is 'that which remains' (*AL* II:9)

What remains? What has happened? We realize that 'every man and every woman is a star' (*AL* I:3).

We look around at our broader heritage. We are staring at our lady Nuit's body. We are not in the dark; we are much closer to her now. What appeared to be specks of light from the little planet are now blazing like other splendid suns, and these are indeed our brothers and sisters, whose essential and starry nature we had never seen or realized before. These are the 'remains' of those we thought we'd abandoned.

There's plenty of space here. Everyone follows their true path. Everything is joyful.

Now, if you want to go back to the old aeon's perspective, you can. But remember that those around you are suns and stars, not shivering slaves. If you are unwilling to be a king yourself, recognize that they have the same right to kingship as you do, whenever you accept it.

And the moment you desire to do so, you have only to remember this – look at things from the point of view of the sun.

BUILDING THE ASTRAL TEMPLE

It's time to introduce fully one new element of the practice: the building of the **astral temple.**

Instead, we will go back to put our focus on the basics of magick, that is, breathing, visualizing, and *being present in the here and the now* to allow the ongoing strengthening of the body of light and the gradual transference of consciousness in it, to allow for the famed 'astral travel'.

You will quickly realize that, at first, it will look and feel way less glamorous than what you might have read about. However, I promise you will be travelling to places way more incredible than the fantastic accounts you might have chanced upon if you stick to the practices in this book without rushing anything.

NOTES FOR AN ASTRAL ATLAS

One of the most alluring appendices of *Magick in Theory and Practice*, this short text describes Crowley's theory of the astral plane and how to visit it.

To keep it as simple as possible, since going into this subject would require a book of its own, Crowley theorizes that, following the Qabalistic emanation model mapped out in the Tree of Life, everything is part of the godhead. This is how we can travel through the planes: we are already there. We simply need to access that specific frequency of communication.

He also makes an essential point by stating that it is impossible to communicate with an independent intelligence – which he deems to be the real object of astral research – if 'one allows one's imagination to surround one with courtiers of one's own creation'.

Astral travel is not so much a way to experience other realities but rather a way inward to discover your true nature. The starting point is where you are standing right now – just vibrating on a different frequency than your physical sense can perceive. It's time to experience Malkuth.

QUEENDOM

Before embarking on this journey, I want to thank hermeticist Rawn Clark for his seminal book *The Eight Temples Meditation Project*, which helped me immensely to understand this whole astral thing. The following pathworking is inspired by his.

Malkuth is generally translated as 'kingdom', but Clark makes the point that maybe 'queendom' is more accurate: this is since the *shekinah*, the Qabalistic divine feminine, is said to be residing here, in the physical world. Those familiar with the concept of the divine Sophia descending onto the world might see some correspondences there.

This is the realm of ordinary, waking consciousness and day-to-day interactions with our physical environment. While its planetary symbol is Earth, it's not entirely correct to say that Malkuth is our physical planet. Rather, it is symbolic refraction of Earth onto the astral plane and a point of interface between the material realm and the astral. This point of intersection is very dynamic, and we will use this dynamism fully.

REACHING THE GATEWAY

Find a private spot where you are confident you will not be interrupted, and situate yourself comfortably. Thoroughly relax your body. Focus on the natural rhythm of your breathing. Let go of all mundane concerns. Access a state of presence by flowing the *prana* in and out of your body.

Close your eyes and visualize this sigil:

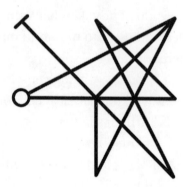

As you do, vibrate[12] the mantra **VOCON HELEMIFATRS**[13] 11 times, taking time to fully regulate inhalation and exhalation of *prana*.

Slowly, let the sigil fade. Then, with your mind's eye, observe the surroundings. You find yourself in a desert, under the night sky. Countless stars illuminate the scene, and you recognize the arched form of the Milky Way. The ancient Egyptians called her Nuit.

---

[12]   Vibration is a consistent, repeated, rhythmic pattern. Mantras are 'vibrated' since they are meant to symbolize the very rhythm of the universe we are looking to harmonize with.

[13]   This sigil and mantra are of my own making, and have been used extensively within my group as beacon and key for the astral temple you are now trying to access. The shape of the sigil reminds me of an energy pylon, and I always found it to be particularly apt!

You start to see the outlines of a cave entrance. A curtain is drawn across the door, bearing a specific symbol. Focus on this symbol and picture it as clearly as you can.

You now say: 'Adonai, please guide me to Malkuth.'

Answering your plea, the Hebrew letters אֲדֹנָי (ADNI) appear at the bottom of the curtain. Visualize the letters in shiny white light. A soft light glows within the cave. You take a moment to acknowledge the experience, draw the curtain aside and enter the cave.

Before you stretches a tunnel. It seems natural, but you notice a chequered pavement on the floor. There are ten tiles, alternating in black and white, and you instantly realize it will take 30 steps to cover it all. With the starlight filtering in, you seem to see some unlit torches mounted on the walls. Before you proceed, consider its features carefully and build a stable image.

Ten steps in, and a torch lights up on your right. You stop and take notice of the torch. Aim to experience it with all your senses: see it, hear it, smell it, feel its heat. Before continuing, look around and reaffirm your visualization of the tunnel from your current position.

Another ten steps in, and a second torch lights up on the left wall. As you've done before, take the time to examine it and then reorient your visualization.

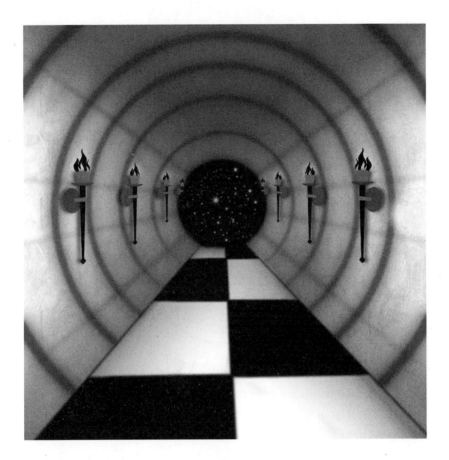

Another ten steps in, you finally arrive at a stairway leading to a vaulted chamber. Again, there are ten steps: count them off to yourself as you climb.

Finally, you stand in the Malkuth temple, facing the eastern quarter. The temple is built of hewn stone, and the floor is translucent marble. In the centre of the temple is a double-cubed altar: the bottom is made of many multi-coloured squares, while the top is adorned by mystic symbols. The temple's four walls are carved in archways, covered by curtains made of gossamer silk.

Beyond each curtain, windows give vistas to the elemental worlds. You take some time to approach them one by one. As you do so, four creatures emerge from the windows.

In the east, an airy sylph. In the south, a fiery salamander. In the west, a watery undine. And finally, in the north, an earthy gnome.

They give you their name in turn and share some of the essential nature of their element. You listen in silence, and you focus on their lessons. They teach you that to fully gain mastery over the elemental chaos, you must learn to invoke the power and authority of the four archangels and master the pentagram.

Once you have spent some time with each of them, they disappear from sight.

You take one last look at the temple of Malkuth, knowing inside your heart that now you will be able to return here at will. You move back into the tunnel and return to your ordinary consciousness.

You have work to do.

DAILY PRACTICE (DURATION: 1 MONTH)

✪ Practice the fourfold breathing constantly. If you cannot do anything else, just sit quietly for ten minutes a day, observing your breathing.

✪ Establish presence by recognizing the elements inside you, taking special care of observing your thoughts, your feelings or emotions, your rush of passions or creative impulses, and the changes in your body sensations.

✪ Practise the solar adorations each day, without fail.

✪ Every Sunday, access the astral temple of Malkuth. Try to memorize the sequence, strengthening your visualization skills.

ERECTING THE SUPERSTRUCTURE

CHAPTER 3

ERECTING THE SUPERSTRUCTURE

You should be familiar with your sensations, feelings, and thoughts by now.

Once you begin to practise concentration and meditation, it will be as though all the forces within yourself arise in open revolt against this discipline. The exercise will activate old memories and infantile feelings and may disturb you unless you have achieved a high degree of self-awareness. In acquiring this awareness, much of the value of the former exercises comes into play.

The previous exercises should have resulted in acquiring some degree of peace and quiet. Instead, a sense of well-being will start to manifest within yourself. This calmness is needed for you to open up and receive the influx of the astral light from the divine at will. You can think of it as a quicker way to access the same source you are connecting with while practising the solar adorations. Practising them has awakened you to this link. Now you must learn to continually fuel it. Even though no progress seems to be made at first, and no response is felt, you should never be discouraged.

You must understand that, at this stage, you have no way to gauge your progress. But, most importantly, you must give up the hope for fast results. I always keep repeating it – and will keep on doing so throughout this book as well – that taking up a magick practice is akin to training for and then running a marathon – not a sprint. The concept of expecting something to happen quickly must be given up quickly.

DHARANA: WILL THROUGH CONCENTRATION

By training concentration – also called *dharana*, another of the eight limbs of yoga – you will also start working on the development of the magical will. Most of the practices waiting for you ahead will hinge on using these inner faculties.

You must have already discovered what a menagerie lives inside yourself. When I ask you at the very beginning to take notice of your thoughts, emotions, and body sensations without interfering with their movement, it will show you something of the nature of your inner world. You should not ignore, fight, or suppress them. Attempting to do so will heighten their intrusion and give them even more power. By silently observing, watching, and taking note of their interactions, you will diminish their hold on you and start developing concentration. We have to learn patience to combat restlessness.

Our mind has a natural tendency to adopt habits, like waking up at a specific time of the morning and eating breakfast, lunch, and dinner at certain times, not because we are hungry but because we have become used to doing so. We can use this fact to assist us in our practice of concentration.

First, choose a given time during the day. Then, practise at that same time, even if it is only for ten minutes, but always at precisely the same time of the day, in the same room, and in the same chair or posture. What you are really doing here is tracking your time with a conditioned reflex so that you will find it much easier to concentrate at this time than at any other. In fact, if you try to skip the exercise at that hour, you will likely experience a sense of unease or anxiety, forcing you to engage with the practices.

A particular room arranged as a temple would be ideal, of course. Also, burning a stick of incense or lighting a candle may assist in getting the vibe just right. However, if those are not available, don't worry. These are merely conveniences and nothing more.

THE POWER OF THE MANTRA

Another simple but powerful practice for slowing down the mind's chatter is mantra. A mantra is simply a word or a phrase, often of a spiritual or magical nature, which is repeated over and over again until it is taken up by the mind itself. Thus a mechanical aid of concentration is perfected, which can then be used to further the predetermined goals.

Let me suggest the Hindu mantra *Om Nama Ha Shivaya Om*. It has eight syllables, which can be broken down into two lines of four beats each:

Om Na Ma Ha
Shi Va Ya Om

This mantra should be memorized first and then recited mentally in time with the breathing. For example, on the inhalation, say *Om Na Ma Ha*, and on the exhalation: *Shi Va Ya Om*. I told you that breathing was crucial for these practices after all!

Once you automate the process without overthinking it, you can start reflecting more on what the phrases mean and what passion they have or can be endowed with. This emotional force directs the mind decisively toward maintaining the mantra until the concentration is an ever-present fact. In time, this *dharana* concentration can be turned on and off until it becomes a faculty available at will. If you are wondering, the mantra above means 'O salutations to the auspicious one!' or 'Adoration to Lord Shiva'.

THE HOLIEST OF MANTRAS

You might still wonder where those Egyptian deities connected to the stations of the sun came from. Despite my continuous remarks against overthinking, I am sure you haven't been able to get rid of that curiosity yet.

Crowley, like many other students of the mysteries, considered Egypt – or Khem, to use its Egyptian name – as the source of the light of initiation. In a later chapter, we will analyze these ideas deeper, but for now, let me give you another mantra to use in your practices:

A Ka Dua
O High One!
Tuf Ur Bi-u
May he be praised!
Bi Aà Chefu
The one great of power!
Dudu Nur Af An Nuteru
The spirit great of dignity, who places fear of himself among the gods!

Crowley considered it the holiest of mantras since he derived it while establishing the esoteric philosophy of Thelema.

The timing of this one is a little trickier, so I recorded it for you to listen to, see the QR code and URL at the end of the book.

DRAWING DOWN THE LIGHT

As soon as you've experimented with the techniques of concentration described above (let's say, having practised them for at least a week), you can move on to the next one.

Once again, an early attempt at drawing down the astral light and reaffirming your connection with the divine, the **middle pillar** practice is based on the symbolism of the Qabalistic Tree of Life. First, you imagine bright light descending and flowing through the body's central axis, marked by a series of energy centres (called *chakras*[14] in Sanskrit), and visualize specific colours and vibrations of the associated divine names activating these centres. Then this light is circulated or directed into a particular flow pattern throughout your subtle body, creating a sort of shell and the first layer of your body of light.

There are countless variations of this practice, and it's believed that the first to codify it was Israel Regardie working with material from the Hermetic Order of the Golden Dawn. However, the one you will study here has a specific flavour.

THE THELEMIC MIDDLE PILLAR

There are nearly as many Thelemic variations of this practice as of the Qabalistic version. The one I am presenting here was taught to me by one of my teachers. While researching and cross-checking my sources for this book, I realized the original author is magician and writer Jason Augustus Newcomb. I want to thank him for giving me the green light to republish it in the present book with some minor personal variations.

---

[14] Literally 'wheel' or 'circle'.

TRADITIONAL MIDDLE PILLAR

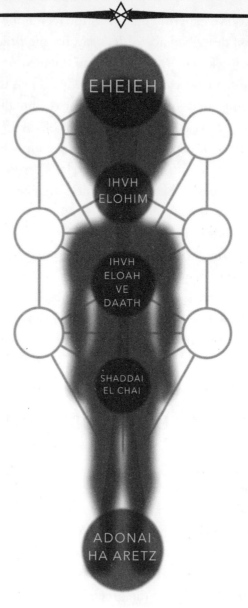

THELEMIC MIDDLE PILLAR

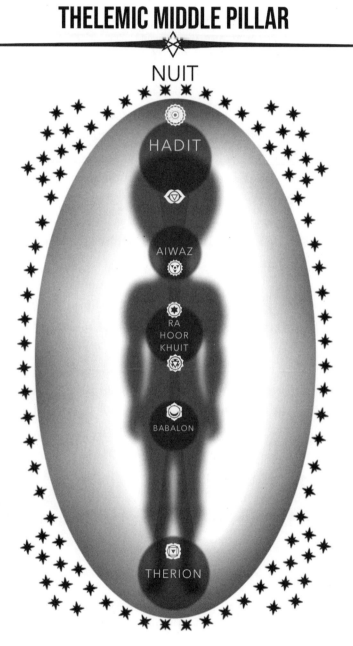

Above: The energies invoked in the Thelemic middle pillar

1.   You may sit or lie down flat. Take a few minutes to relax your body and establish a breathing pattern. The classic fourfold breath battery of inhaling for four seconds, holding for four seconds, then slowly exhaling for four seconds, and holding it for four is perfect. As discussed previously, you aim to achieve presence.

2.   Close your eyes, and become aware of the void behind your closed eyes. It extends infinitely in all directions. You may begin to notice flashes of light or stars, but continue concentrating on the infinity around you. Now, slowly and powerfully **vibrate** the name **NUIT**. Imagine the expanse of infinity behind your closed eyes to be you as you do this. You are that infinity. **Vibrate NUIT five more times, all the time expanding your awareness.**

3.   Now breathe into the uppermost point of your head. Imagine that to be your apparatus for breathing. Concentrate all of your breath's energy – *prana* – at the crown of your head. This experience may seem tenuous at first, but don't worry about that for now; soon, it will feel much more potent. Continuing to breathe into your crown, visualize a sphere or star of bright white shining light just above your head. It's about the size of a tennis ball. Radiation should pour out of it as if it were a miniature sun – your own personal sun.

4.   Inhale, intensely concentrating on the breath filling up the star above your head. As you exhale, **vibrate** the name **HADIT**. Watch and feel the star growing in brilliance. **Repeat this process five more times.**

5.   Relax for a few moments and feel the energy pulsing above your head.

6.   Now exhale. Push down a shaft of white light through your head from the star above you. Direct it to your throat.

7.   Begin breathing energy down the shaft into your throat, always beginning at the star above your head. Now visualize a second sphere or star in the centre of your throat. Inhale,

intensely concentrating on the descending energy into your throat. As you exhale, **vibrate** the name **AIWAZ**. Watch and feel the star brighten. **Repeat this process five more times.**

8. Relax and feel the energy pulsing through your head and throat.

9. Now exhale. Push the shaft of white light down past your throat from the star in your throat. Direct it to the area around your heart and solar plexus.

10. Breathe energy down the shaft into your throat and chest, always beginning at the star above your head. Now visualize a third sphere or star in the centre of your chest. Inhale, intensely concentrating on the descending energy into your chest, and as you exhale, **vibrate** the name **RA-HOOR-KHUIT**. Visualize the star brighten and become more brilliant as you do this. **Repeat this process five more times.**

11. Relax and observe your body, noticing any changes, and feel the pulsation of the energy.

12. Now exhale. Push the shaft of white light down through your chest from the star above you. Direct it to your pelvic area.

13. Breathe energy down the shaft into your throat and your chest. And then down to your pelvis, always beginning at the star above your head. Now visualize a fourth sphere or star around your genitals. Inhale, intensely concentrating on the descending energy into your genitals, and **vibrate** the name **BABALON** as you exhale. Feel the star growing in brilliance as you do this. **Repeat this process five more times.**

14. Relax and feel this powerful flow of energy.

15. Now exhale. Push the shaft of white light down through your genitals from the star above you to your feet.

16. Breathe energy down the shaft into your throat and your chest. And through your genitals, and down to your feet, always beginning at the star above your head. Now visualize a fifth sphere or star beneath your feet. Inhale, intensely concentrating on the descending energy into your feet, and **vibrate** the name

THERION as you exhale. Feel the star growing in brilliance as you do this. **Repeat this process five more times.**

17. Relax and observe your body again, notice whatever is happening there, and feel the radiating energy. Then, maintaining the downward flow as much as possible, focus your attention back on the star above your head.

18. Now exhale. Push a sphere of light and energy from the star above your head. Direct it down the left side of your body to the star beneath your feet. Next, inhale, and bring it back up your right side to the star above your head, forming a circle of light around you. **Repeat this five times or until it seems solid.**

19. Now exhale. Push a sphere of light down the front of your body to the star beneath your feet. Inhale, and bring it back up the rear of your body to the star above your head, forming another circle of light. **Repeat this process five more times.**

20. Relax for a few moments and feel these energy pathways as vividly as possible.

21. Focus your attention on the star beneath your feet. Inhale and bring a spiralling shaft of light swirling up around your body and to the star above your head. While exhaling, visualize a firework-like explosion of light that rains gently upon you. It flows into the star beneath your feet. **Repeat this process five more times.**

22. Now, you are surrounded by an egg of energy, pulsing through and around your body. You are in a cocoon, and you will now begin to transform. Within you, there is a bird of prey, a golden hawk. Feel your face grow more streamlined as a beak forms. Feel your arms slowly transform into wings, golden feathers appearing all over your body. Then, when you feel ready, break free from the egg in your golden hawk body, and soar into the infinite emptiness beyond. Return only when ready. Soar for as long as you like.

23. Open your eyes. Put your right forefinger to your lips and **vibrate silently** (that is, in your head) the name **HOOR-PAAR-KRAAT**

One of the best ways to learn this practice is to have someone read it to you, giving you time to let the images form in your mind's eye and concentrate on the pathways of energy flowing through you and receiving the astral light. A common name for these guided meditations is pathworking, especially when receiving visions of the 22 paths of the Tree of Life.

Once again, I recorded it for you, see the QR code and URL at the end of the book.

THE RITUALS OF THE PENTAGRAM

The pentagram rituals are some of the earliest tools devised to help the magician bring order to the chaos in the elemental realm. The goal of performing a pentagram ritual is to establish yourself at the very centre of a new, enchanted universe. However, for the magician to do this, they must magically and symbolically identify their participation and alignment in the spiritual world.

This means that saying these words and performing these visualizations and gestures requires concentrating on all the multiple correspondences, energies, and movements at once. By the end of this chapter, you will have a good idea on how to do this.

The first time you learn these rituals, you will have to go through all the movements many times to establish muscle memory. You should aim to memorize words and gestures without giving them much thought. While you are concentrating on learning the moves, you won't be aware of all the magical implications in your performance. So it's common for people to forget how powerful this whole process is because they are still unfamiliar with these rituals at this stage. The truth is that once correctly performed and integrated, the pentagram rituals are genuine and authentic invocations. You can also see them as a form of 'hermetic meditation' that works wonders once it's correctly integrated into your magical routine.

By now, you will have noticed a trend in rituals. First of all, you force yourself to do something that does not make much sense – at least in terms of mundane logic. Then you keep doing it, and as you do, you start to understand it – you gain spiritual insight into what the Greeks called *gnosis*. You have seen it happen already with the Solar Adorations, and with the Astral Temple.

You can spend a lot of time and energy trying to figure out the structure of that language and its permutations – but there is danger in that. You can easily get caught up in this process, and you end up ignoring the semantics of the language. What I mean by this is that you should aim to strike a precise balance between overthinking all the symbology and not caring about it at all. With this in mind, when you consider a ritual and its purposes, you must ask yourself not just why the symbols were placed the way they are, but also the spiritual significance behind every juxtaposition.

When people are first introduced to pentagram rituals, they usually pay most attention to the pentagram as a symbol. But they miss out on the significance of other features, including both body movements and visualizations. You cannot accurately talk about these rituals without considering how these visualizations and movements define the space you perform the rituals in and how the pentagram is used as a component of broader ritual action.

To understand this better, let's start with the **Lesser Ritual of the Pentagram** (abbreviated to LRP). This is the most basic pentagram ritual, and the one you will end up using the most. As you might have already guessed, it's the one attributed to the element of Earth, and so you can deduce that there are pentagram rituals for each element, both in banishing and invoking form.

You can break down the structure of LRP into:

- The Qabalistic cross
- The pentagrams
- The four elemental quarters
- The cross and circle conjoined

We can assume that this ritual was created by S L MacGregor Mathers,[15] one of the founders and chiefs of the Hermetic Order of the Golden Dawn. However, it would seem that the main inspiration comes from Éliphas Lévi's *Transcendental Magic*.

OVERVIEW OF THE
LESSER RITUAL OF THE PENTAGRAM

Before discussing all of its distinct elements, let's look at the ritual – specifically as presented in Aleister Crowley's *Liber O vel Manus et Sagittae*. Here it is:

Start by facing east.
Touch your forehead, and then say **Ateh** (Hebrew for 'Unto Thee')
Then touch your breast, saying **Malkuth** ('The Kingdom'),

---

[15] Samuel Liddell MacGregor Mathers (8 or 11 January 1854–5 or 20 November 1918), born Samuel Liddell Mathers, was a British occultist. He is primarily known as one of the founders of the Hermetic Order of the Golden Dawn. He became so synonymous with the order that many observed in retrospect that 'the Golden Dawn was MacGregor Mathers.' (*Wikipedia*)

LESSER RITUAL OF THE PENTAGRAM

Above: The Lesser Ritual of the Pentagram and the
angelic forces invoked by it

Touch your right shoulder, saying **ve-Geburah** ('and the Power'),

Touch your left shoulder, saying **ve-Gedulah** ('and the Glory'),

Finally, clasp your hands upon the breast, saying **le-Olahm, Amen** ('To the Ages, Amen').

Take a step toward the east, and make a pentagram (that of Earth, see below) with the proper weapon (usually the wand). Vibrate **IHVH** (pronounced *Yê-ho-wau-he*).

Walk in a circular motion toward the south, and repeat the same, but vibrate **ADNI** (pronounced *Ad-oh-nay*).

Walk in a circular motion toward the west, and repeat the same, but vibrate **AHIH** (pronounced *Ee-hay-yay*).

Walk in a circular motion toward the north, repeat the same, but vibrate **AGLA** (pronounce *Ahg-lah*).

Now extend the arms in the form of a cross, and then say with a clear voice:

Before me Raphael;

Behind me Gabriel;

On my right, Michael.

On my left, Auriel;

All around me flames the pentagram,

While in the column stands the six-rayed star.

You will close the ritual by repeating the Qabalistic cross and retreating in silence.

The structure of the ritual remains the same both in the banishing and invoking forms, only the pentagrams change. Consequently, this ritual has eight permutations: four pentagrams of the elements, with two forms of each:

INVOKING
BANISHING

EARTH
GREEN

AIR
YELLOW

WATER
BLUE

FIRE
RED

SPIRIT

ACTIVE
SPIRIT

PASSIVE
SPIRIT

Above: The banishing and invoking forms of the pentagrams.
Take note of the various signs attributed to each element.
You first saw them in the solar adoration.

You will use a banishing when you want to remove excessive elemental energy from your body of light and your immediate surroundings. Conversely, using an invoking form will bring more elemental energy in your space, supercharging it.

SOUND

In the Thelemic tradition I was personally taught, the words provided in fourfold capital letters (IHVH and so on) in the text provided above are vibrated using a unique intonation. At specific places in the ritual, the vocal vibration directs and raises the *prana* through the body of light. This is done by intoning what we call divine names. Bear in mind that there are different methods for vibrating divine names, some of which are used alongside visualizations. Whichever way this is done, though, the voice needs to be projected deeply, loudly, clearly, and mindfully.

This is how the divine names are pronounced:

- Ye-ho-wau-he
- Ad-oh-nay
- Ee-hay-yay
- Ahg-lah

AGLA, in Qabalistic terms, is called a *notariqon*, which is a word created through the use of acronyms. AGLA, for example, is constructed from the first letter of each word in *Atah Gibor le-Ohlahm Adonai*, which means 'Thou art mighty unto the ages Adonai.' You can, if you wish, say the statement in full facing north rather than abbreviate. Mathers called these four names **tetragrammatic names** because they share the same fourfold structure as the elements themselves. The four names represent the unity of the divine name, symbolizing quintessence, the fifth element of spirit, which expresses itself through four elements. This is why these four elements are placed at the four quarters – to represent the four aspects of manifested reality. This is what forms the primary structural meaning of the ritual.

IMAGE

Throughout history, the ritual has been associated with different visualizations. These differences exist between groups and communities, and even individuals. Because the visualizations are many, I will provide you with standard suggestions. Experiment with any of them, and tweak them to make your own.

While making the Qabalistic cross, imagine an energy current as a flaming and radiant white light going through your body and crossing your chest. Bring to mind each pentagram as it is being drawn. You can visualize it either as a white light or in the colour that matches the element in question (Air: yellow; Fire: red; Water: blue; Earth: green). Next, make a white circle around the perimeter at heart level as you transition between quarters.

THE QABALISTIC CROSS

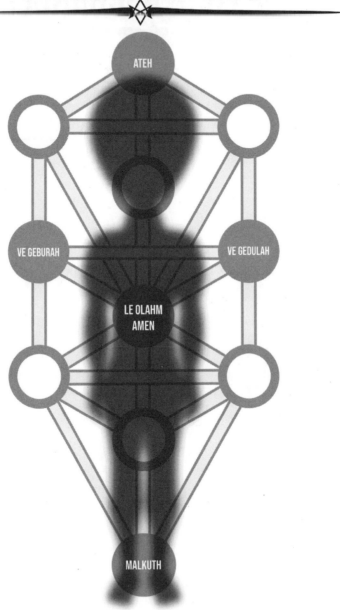

Finally, visualize (imagine) the archangels surrounding the circle as you invoke them to conclude the whole procedure.

THE FOUR ARCHANGELS

You can think of the archangels as angelic, giant-statured figures wearing robes coloured according to their element and carrying different weapons to symbolize it:

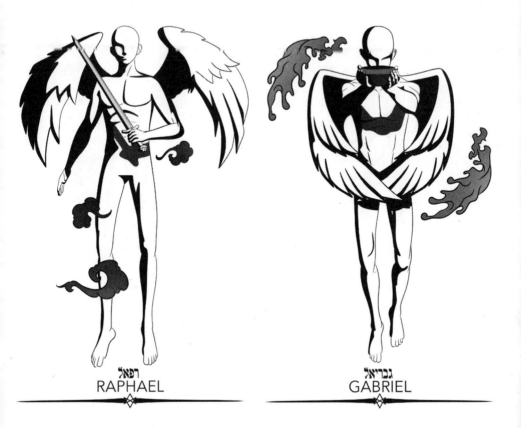

רפאל
RAPHAEL

גבריאל
GABRIEL

Above and overleaf: The four archangels, bearing the four elemental weapons

- Raphael holds a sword for Air
- Gabriel brings a cup, representing Water
- Michael is pictured with a lance (representing a wand) to stand for Fire
- Auriel has a disk (also called a paten) representing Earth

מיכאל
MICHAEL

אוריאל
AURIEL

WAIT A MINUTE — ANGELS?
I THOUGHT THIS WAS THELEMA!

Even when working in a Thelemic paradigm, we can't ignore
the magical systems that came before it. At least, not all of them.
There is a clear intimation in *The Book of the Law* – the core text
of Thelema – that reminds us that, while some old rituals are
abrogated, others are superseded.

   You can think of it as installing new software while continuing
to use a couple of trusty old apps that still do the job just fine.

The work with angels and archangels in ceremonial magick is one such case of maintaining old magical systems. There will come a time when, after having mastered these introductory rituals, you will move on to something that *looks* and *feels* more Thelemic, such as the *Star Ruby* or the *Mark of the Beast*. But before getting there, you must prove your proficiency in the foundational work first.

There is another reason why working with the angels is indispensable for beginners. The word 'angel' comes from the Greek word ἄγγελος (*angelos*), which means literally 'messenger'. So, you can think of them as layers of consciousness of the essential infrastructure of our perceived reality. We are surrounded by angels at all times, who constantly move information across all layers of manifestation. It should be clear why learning to work with them magically is of great practical use.

Traditionally, the angels are organized in ranks. And in turn, each rank is governed by one archangel. The four we invoke in the rituals of the pentagram have specific dominion over the elements of the quarters and have specific attributions to the sephiroth of the Tree of Life.

DO I NEED MAGICAL TOOLS?

If you like, you can perform these rituals using wands or ritual daggers to draw the pentagram figures. This action has many symbolic implications, which you should, in time, learn from studying the system of correspondences mapped on the Qabalistic Tree of Life, which we covered earlier. For example, everything I have outlined so far can be expanded this way, according to Aleister Crowley:

The dagger represents the element of Air. It is used to symbolize Yetzirah, Ruach, and Tiphareth, which lies at the centre of this layer of the Tree of Life. And so, we can surmise that the dagger acts to summon Yetziratic energy in the ritual. The goal is to equilibrate the elements in the Knowledge and Conversation of the Holy Guardian Angel.

The dagger can be replaced by the sword to switch the emphasis on the sephirah Geburah most strongly. This is the fifth sephirah. It represents the pentagram itself with its five points. But also the active will, spiritual chivalry, and the disruption of unbalanced forces through the True Will. Finally, the sword represents the lightning flash on the Tree of Life. This is the pure active, creative energy of spirit encompassing all of the sephiroth.

As you can see, simply changing the tool you use will give a different twist to the whole ritual.

Obviously, you can't expect to be able to conduct the ritual at this level of complexity straight away. However, this is the level of engagement and layering of ideas and concepts that a true initiate or adept needs to achieve. This level of complexity is what is needed for these rituals to work to their full potential.

HORUS TO THE RESCUE

All of the above said, you can also perform this ritual with no tools. Simply vibrate the divine names of the quarters while making the sign of the enterer, and then make the sign of silence at the end of each quarter.

THE SIGN OF THE ENTERER

Make the projecting sign, otherwise called the enterer, by stepping forward with one foot and thrusting your arms out at eye level. Make sure that your palms stay flat and your index fingers are extended. This movement symbolizes you projecting your divine will into the universe as magical energy. You are establishing yourself as the centre of light in the cosmos. According to *The Book of the Law*, I:3: 'Every man and every woman is a star.'

Some people also refer to this sign as the sign of Horus, being associated with its active, martial form: Ra-Hoor-Kuit. According to some sources, Horus represents the Holy Guardian Angel's power, so this sign symbolizes the angel acting through the magician's agency.

SIGN OF THE ENTERER
SIGN OF HORUS

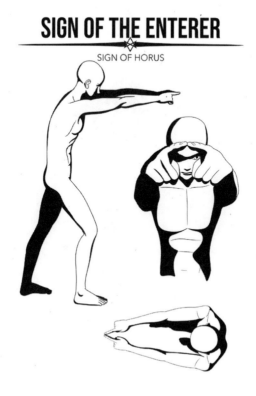

THE SIGN OF SILENCE

Make the sign of silence by stepping back your extended foot so that your feet are back in a parallel position. Drop your left arm to the side and place your right index finger on your closed lips. Hold the other fingers in a loose fist. The idea is to seal the energy current that has been released by the projecting sign. The sign of silence represents a magician at rest in gnosis. If the projecting sign is a sign of magick, then the sign of silence is a sign of mysticism.

It can also be called the sign of Harpocrates – the baby Horus, Hoor-Paar-Kraat.

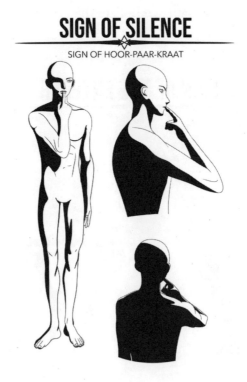

SIGN OF SILENCE

SIGN OF HOOR-PAAR-KRAAT

THE QABALISTIC CROSS

As hinted above, you cannot understand the Qabalistic cross without referring to Éliphas Lévi's writings.

According to him, the cross sign that the Christians adopted is not exclusively theirs. It is a Qabalistic representation of the tetradic balance and oppositions of the elements. He insisted that there are two ways of understanding it – one for the profane and the other for the priests and initiates. He said that the sign of the cross should always come before and after a conjuration of the elements.

The Qabalistic cross is made on the body, in line with the idea that a magician should express all the symbols and meanings described by the ritual. It has two dimensions. The vertical dimension refers to the divine, while the horizontal refers to material existence. You draw the vertical line first because the spirit comes first and extends across all reality planes in our world. Then you describe the horizontal axis, thereby forming a point at its centre where the two axes meet. This point represents the true self – Hadit – which is in the heart. It also describes the place where matter and spirit meet and are united. This is the mystical nothing.

> I am the flame that burns in every heart of man, and in the core of every star. I am Life, and the giver of Life, yet therefore is the knowledge of me the knowledge of death. *(AL II:6)*

The cross is also a representation of the Tree of Life manifested in and on the human body. It expresses the unity of the microcosm and macrocosm. As the *Emerald Tablet* of Hermes Trismegistos puts it, everything below is like everything above, and everything above is like everything below.

In other words, the Tree of Life represents the body of God and aspects of the universe. At the same time, it represents the magician's body and their own aspects. This is the doctrine of *anthropocosmos*, which teaches that the imaginal and physical bodies of the magician represent the body of God.

The first thing you draw is the middle pillar extending from Kether over the head to Malkuth at the feet. The balance of opposites must always come before. It has a greater significance than the duality of the opposing forces that the pillars of severity and mercy represent (indicated by the horizontal plane on the cross.)

WHAT ABOUT AIWASS?

Some traditions add this Thelemic name to the Qabalistic cross and effectively make that fifth element we just discussed. This likely originates from Phyllis Seckler's teachings since it never appears in Crowley's publications. Aiwass, as we will see in due course, is a fundamental figure in Thelemic theology. At one point, Crowley considered it to be the name of his own Holy Guardian Angel, and so equating it with quintessence isn't necessarily wrong.

My suggestion is that for the time being, you keep the ritual as simple as possible: there will come a time to spice it up further.

THE PENTAGRAMS PROPER

There are some symbolic meanings to the form of the pentagram that you can see immediately. The pentagram has five points to represent the four elements plus spirit. You draw it with a single unbroken line to symbolize the unity of the spirit with its elemental forms. The figure is meant to fit in a circle, to show how it all depends on the divine unity. It is shaped like a person to represent the magician himself. It also looks like a traditional star, true to the words of *The Book of the Law* I:3: 'Every man and every woman is a star.'

The five points also stand for the fifth sephirah, Geburah, which represents the active and martial power of the magician over the elements, bound to the service of the Holy Guardian Angel's consciousness. The five points mean the same thing as the elements of the cross do. Again referencing *The Book of the Law*, we hear Nuit, the goddess of the night sky, say that the five-pointed star with a red circle at the middle is her symbol.

As you can see, the pentagram's symbolism is a visual résumé of the whole ritual. So, for example, drawing the pentagram at the four quarters shows the spirit's dominion over the elementals as embodied by the magician.

Usually, specific elements get assigned to the points in the pentagram based on the cross formed in the heavens by the fixed zodiac sign positions.

Above: The pentagram superimposed on the zodiac wheel

Some elements can be banished or invoked based on how you draw the pentagram in relation to the points. As a general rule, if the pentagram is drawn with the first line moving away from the point of a specific element, that element is banished.

The notable exception here is the element of spirit, which we will discuss later when analyzing the **Greater Ritual of the Pentagram**.

THE FOUR QUARTERS

The four quarters refer to four directions to which you apply the pentagrams, the visualizations of the angels, and the divine names. Once again – really hammering the concept in! – these are the four elements. The magician stands in the centre and represents the spirit. Another essential thing to consider is that looking at our preferred map of reality, the Tree of Life, this is the intersection of the paths of Peh and Samekh:

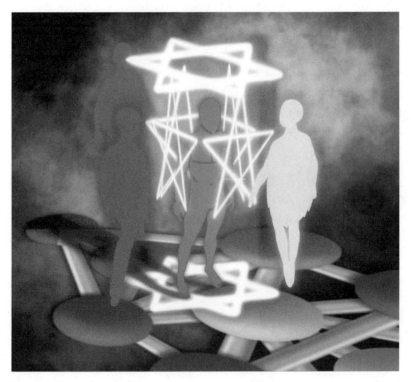

Above: A depiction of the magician performing a pentagram ritual, projected onto the Tree of Life

This is the central key equilibrium point in the A∴A∴[16] Outer College. The ascending aspiration toward Tiphareth along the path of Samekh has to cross the path of Peh. This also happens to correspond with The Tower card in the tarot. The lesson encoded here is that the true initiation of the Holy Guardian Angel cannot be achieved without perfect balance over elemental chaos, as I mentioned at the beginning of this chapter.

This intersection point represents elemental equilibration: the aligning of the phenomenal self's cognitive, physical, emotional, and intentional aspects to the True Will.

At the point of transition for each quadrant, you draw a pentagram, vibrate a divine name, and finally visualize and invoke an archangel. This places the Qabalistic four worlds in equilibrium with each other. The divine name refers to Atziluth, the archangels to Briah, and the way you visualize the pentagrams refers to Yetzirah. The ritual performance in an actual, physical space brings it all down to Assiah.

Once more: pause for a second here to appreciate the complexities hidden in plain sight – both now as you are learning the ritual, and when you will be actually performing it! This is the actual kernel of the magical engine.

---

[16] The A∴A∴ is Crowley's main magical order, and was organized in 1907 as the Thelemic continuation of the Hermetic Order of the Golden Dawn, the teachings of which became its Outer or Introductory College. Its members are dedicated to the advancement of humanity by perfection of the individual on every plane through a graded series of universal initiations. Its initiations are syncretic, unifying the essence of tantra, yoga, and ceremonial magic. The A∴A∴ applies what it describes as mystical and magical methods of spiritual attainment under the structure of the Qabalistic Tree of Life, and aims to research, practise, and teach 'scientific illuminism'. A∴A∴ is often held to stand for Argenteum Astrum, which is Latin for Silver Star. Other explanations for the acronym are given as *Arcana Arcanorum* (Latin: Secret of Secrets), or *Angel and Abyss*. (*Wikipedia*)

THE CROSS AND THE CIRCLE CONJOINED

The cross and the circle symbol is formed by the magician's circular movements about the four quarters.

It is an important symbol in Thelemic magick. It is also the rosy cross of the Rosicrucian movement. According to Crowley, Thelema was supposed to be its final reverberation in the new aeon.

The Thelemic interpretation of the rosy cross symbolizes the union of the object and subject in samadhi and the continued embrace of Nuit and Hadit. The cross represents consciousness and is extended upon the rose (here depicted as the circle) to signify all the possible experiences available to manifestation.

INVOKING AND BANISHING

We have finally arrived at the specific practice you should make yours before everything else. I do realize it took us a bit longer than you were likely expecting. As you certainly must have realized by now, we needed to establish the ideas behind it all.

The first iteration of the Lesser Ritual of the Pentagram is the banishing and invoking of the element Earth. It should be understood as the stand-in for all pentagrams because, traditionally, this element contains the other three. For example, in the *Sepher Yetzirah*, Earth forms when you combine Air,

Fire, and Water. Therefore, the three are considered 'mother' elements. If you are familiar with the Hebrew language (something that will come in handy the more you study magick), you might have noticed that this mirrors the three mother letters *aleph*, *shin* and *mem*. They are, in fact, assigned respectively to those very same elements.

The difference between the banishing and invoking forms is subtle because it is primarily a distinction of emphasis. Invoking brings a current of balanced elemental force into the ritual space. The term itself comes from the Latin *invoco*, 'to call something inside'. In contrast, banishing directs that energy to dissolve and clear any unbalanced forces.

Most of the time, the Lesser Ritual of the Pentagram is used to open up a ritual space by clearing negative energy. Traditionally, it's the banishing form that gets used: this is the well-known **LBRP** (**L**esser **B**anishing **R**itual of the **P**entagram) you might have heard mentioned before.

This is certainly not the only use of these rituals, however. As we saw in the previous chapter, and I emphasised above, each element can be mapped in the psychophysical body of the magician. And, thus, we can use the pentagrams to ease specific issues or exalt qualities.

Feeling sluggish? Banish the element of Earth.
Suffering from anxiety? Banish the element of Air.
Needing a creative boost? Invoke the element of Fire.
Want to kick the blues away? Banish the element of Water.

These are obviously only examples, and it's down to the growing discernment of the magician to map the elements and their own felt experience correctly. Time and constant practice are of the essence here.

DAILY PRACTICE (DURATION: 1 MONTH)

✪ Start by focusing on the pentagram of Earth during the first week. Perform twice a day: invoke the element in the morning, and banish it in the evening.

✪ Keep up with the presence practice introduced in previous chapters. Try doing it for at least 30 minutes a day now. Visualize the breathing (*prana*), creating a layer of energy surrounding your physical body. What colour is it? What's it made of?

✪ From the second week onwards, focus on the other elements in turn: Water, Air, and finally Fire.

✪ Spend some time each day to find the elements in your own body and daily lived experience. Recognize if there is an excess or a lack of each, and correct the imbalance using the correct form of pentagrams. Invoking will correct a deficiency, while banishing will correct an excess.

✪ Remember: these elements make up the building blocks of your magical pyramid, as we discussed previously. The pentagrams allow for the refinement and employment of these building blocks. So take all the time you need to master them: four weeks is only a starting point!

CUTTING CORNERS AND MAGICAL PLATEAUS

CHAPTER 4

CUTTING CORNERS, AND MAGICAL PLATEAUS

Jason's pursuit of the Golden Fleece is a fantastic illustration of the archetypal process of nature referred to in the *Emerald Tablet* of Hermes Trismegistus as 'the operation of the sun', a generation ahead of mythological Cadmus and a generation behind Homer's Ulysses. In Thelemic terms, we see this as the journey toward Heliopolis and the whole union with the angel that opens up the gateways to true magick.

From Nicholas Flamel to Fulcanelli, the greatest alchemical adepts have talked with perfect clarity and infuriating obliqueness about the bench-top laboratory manipulations revealed in the circumstances of Jason's expedition.

Despite being considered by many the 'esoteric psychologist', Carl Gustav Jung confines Jason's Argo to the psychological plane of personality integration. He disregards the experiments adepts conduct in their laboratories. Modern scholars of esotericism, such as Antoine Faivre, keep ignoring this essential part of the royal art, which is concerned with a mix of prayer, research, and actual hands-on labour with the crude matter.

Above: 'ORA, LEGE, LEGE, LEGE, RELEGE, LABORA ET INVENIES', declares the motto of the *Mutus Liber* of 1677: 'Pray, Read, Read, Read, Read Again, and You Shall Find.'

CUTTING CORNERS

So, why did I insist above on the idea of assiduous practice?

One thing I constantly repeated over the years I taught these materials online during the lockdowns and in person is that the aspirant cannot cut corners. This whole experience is a marathon, not a sprint. Rush it, and the only result will be building a temple with no solid foundation, unable to receive your angel. And in turn, it will render you unable to ever work true magick.

Nowadays, we live in flats with partners, children, or even lousy neighbours who would pry on our privacy should we go all out while vibrating the divine names in the pentagram rituals.

I fully understand the need to be relatively quiet – I do. However, vibrating a magical name means sustaining the word through the exhalation of *prana*. You inhale, and on the entire length of the exhalation, you say – *vibrate* – the name or magical formula.

This can indeed be done relatively silently. But not at the very start: you need time and a lot of practice.

When learning, I am afraid there are no corners to cut despite the advice I keep seeing: 'It's ok to do what you can.' I hate to be the bearer of bad news, but it isn't.

You cannot cut corners before you have completely *mastered* a practice.

Does it mean you will have to plan your training in more detail, do it when your partner or children aren't at home (not the most uncomplicated feat today, I am aware)? Yes indeed. But this is the way, as the Mandalorian would say.

If you start cutting corners now, you will fall back on the approach that magick is just *manifestation*, and you must only *want* something to have it. And I would fail my duty as a tutor by allowing you to believe it. There are no shortcuts. It will take a LONG time to master these practices.

And that's how it is.

MAGICAL PLATEAUS

There is a counterpoint to being so dedicated. Despite loving the experience here and remaining committed to it, you might feel like you reached a magical plateau a few weeks or a few months down the line.

The strong currents felt at first start to dry up a little, your excitement wanes as a result, and your practice slips away. You are still here, but all in all, maybe this magick thing is way less grand than you expected it to be.

The good news is that if you are feeling this … **YOU ARE DOING IT RIGHT.**

In *Magick in Theory and Practice* – which, by the end of this book, I am pretty sure will be one of the most quoted! – Crowley introduces us to one fundamental magical formula. He calls it the formula of IAO, owing to its name from the Greek Ἰάω, an earlier form of the Tetragrammaton IHVH.

Crowley tells us that IAO is essentially the formula of yoga or meditation.

At the start of meditation practice, there is always a quiet pleasure and a gentle natural growth; one takes a lively interest in the work; it seems easy; one is quite pleased to have started. This stage represents **Isis**, and if this stage is missing, one is not working correctly.

It is eventually followed by melancholy, exhaustion, and a dislike for one's job. Even the simplest activities become almost too hard to accomplish. Such impotence causes anxiety and despair in the psyche. The depth of this hatred is difficult to comprehend for those who have not experienced it. This is the period of **Apophis** and has often been described as the **dark night of the soul**. Remember that this is a process you will encounter many times.

WHAT IS A MAGICAL FORMULA?

A magical formula is a word that is thought to have special magical properties. They are words the meaning of which reflect ideas and levels of comprehension that are frequently difficult to convey through other forms of speech or writing. It is a short way of communicating extremely abstract information via the medium of a word or phrase.

These words frequently have no inherent significance in and of themselves. When the formula is deconstructed, each individual letter may correspond to a universal notion existing in the system in which it appears.

Additionally, in grouping certain letters together, one can display meaningful sequences considered valuable (such as spiritual hierarchies or initiatory stages).

A formula's potency is understood and made usable by the magician only through prolonged meditation on its levels of meaning. Once these have been interiorized by the magician, they may then use the formula to maximum effect.

It is followed by the emergence of **Osiris** rather than Isis. The ancient situation is not restored; rather, a new and higher condition is established, one made possible only by the metaphorical death we have just experienced.

And so here you have IAO completed: Isis, Apophis, Osiris. We will find them again soon while working with the hexagram rituals.

This was taught by the alchemists as well. The starting material of their transmutations was simple and rudimentary, yet natural. Then, after several phases, the black dragon arrived, and from it arose the pure and flawless gold.

Take a look at the earliest tarot decks, and you will see that The Magician card is a juggler: we literally strive to keep the universe itself in perfect balance. And that begins by learning to juggle the strong alchemical tides in our own praxis.

If you feel like you have hit a plateau, rejoice: you are doing it right. What comes next is possibly the most critical lesson in honing your magical will: learn to muster the strength to keep going.

REACHING THE PINNACLE

CHAPTER 5

REACHING THE PINNACLE

A poignant question often arises: 'What precisely does a Thelemite do?'

Many answers could be found to this question. Crowley repeatedly stated that there is a single primary definition of the object of all magical rituals. It is the uniting of the microcosm with the macrocosm. As a result, the supreme ritual is the invocation of the Holy Guardian Angel, or, in mystic terms, union with God. All other magical rituals are exceptions to this general rule.

The danger of ceremonial magick is that magicians will naturally tend to engage with those practices that most strongly appeal to them, so their natural excess in that direction will still be further exaggerated. Therefore, before beginning their magical work, they should endeavour to map out their own being and arrange their practices in such a way as to redress the balance.

And so, what do Thelemites *do*?

They strive to reach union with God, the Knowledge and Conversation with the Holy Guardian Angel, with every tool they can master. And that's what we have been doing so far.

I am telling you this because in these years, magick, witchcraft, hoodoo, spell crafting, and many other practices have become Instagram-friendly and Twitter-worthy. However, the consistent approach to making it all palatable and easily digestible is to find an increasingly easier way to break them down to the most elemental components.

And so, in general, witches brew herbal teas. Hoodoo practitioners dress candles. Chaotes climax over sigils. And ceremonial magicians vibrate often poorly understood Hebrew words over pentagrams.

A Thelemite does all of that and more. Because each willed action is an act of magick toward the union with God. You will decide your particular flavour: Crowley was a ceremonial magician, owing to his background rooted in theosophy, Freemasonry, and the Hermetic Order of the Golden Dawn. I still like a lot of it, but, over the years, I came to distil my practice and make it less bombastic.

But the moment you have fully set yourself toward discovering your True Will and living following the law of liberty, you and only you will decide what to do.

SPIRIT, THE QUINTESSENTIAL FIFTH ELEMENT

With the term astral light, we refer to a metaphysical concept that symbolizes the connection with the divine – that is, the Holy Guardian Angel. Several practices we have experimented with so far are squarely aimed at receiving it and using it to become first aware of and then strengthen our own body of light.

Éliphas Lévi used it to refer to the medium of all light, energy, and movement, following the theory of the luminiferous ether commonly held in the 19th century. In his view, the astral light was a fluidic life force that filled all space and living beings. At that time, this was a rather common theory in fact, and the astral light was rather referred to as the ether. This was considered to be the life force that filled everything and that bound every living being.

Writing of the astral light, Lévi said that:

there exists in nature a force infinitely exceeding that of steam, a force that would enable the man capable of seizing and directing it to change the face of the world. The ancients knew this force: it consists of a Universal Agent whose supreme law is equilibrium and whose direction is directly related to the great arcanum of transcendental magic. Through the use of this agent, one can change the exact order of the seasons, produce the phenomenon of day in the middle of the night, enter instantaneously into contact with the farthest ends of the Earth, and see events on the other side of the world, as Apollonius of Tyana did, heal or attack at a distance, and confer on one's speech universal success and influence. This agent, barely glimpsed by the groping disciples of Mesmer, is nothing other than the First Matter of the Great Work of the medieval adepts.[17]

He and Aleister Crowley considered it one and the same as the quintessential fifth element of the alchemists – spirit.

It should be evident now that all your work so far has been aimed at activating this fifth element in you. You started by focusing on your breathing, the source of your terrestrial life. Then, you studied a convenient map of reality and became acquainted with the lexicon of its many correspondences. Next, you honed your concentration to become able to invoke the visible expression of the godhead by following the course of the sun in the sky, even when you can't see it. You became a ceremonial magician with the pathworking of the middle pillar first. Then by using the lesser pentagrams, you declared yourself the very centre of your own universe and ordained the elements around you in their rightful place.

---

[17] Éliphas Lévi, *Dogme et ritual de la Haute Magic*, translated as *Transcendental Magic*.

THE SPHINX OF THE ADEPTS

In other words, we could say that you dared to see the world in a different light, you sought and accrued knowledge, and you kept silent while working diligently through these practices. Then, finally, you start seeing the fruits of establishing your will in the world.

To dare, to will, to know, to keep silence: these are the four powers of the sphinx, and through them, you unlock the spirit and the final power: to go.

THE FIVE POWERS OF THE SPHINX

Above: The sphinx of the adepts and its five powers

A sphinx is a creature created from many parts but consistently contains a lion's body and a human head. The sphinx of the adepts is made of the head of a man, the torso and front paws of a lion, the rear end of a bull and the wings of the eagle. Each of these parts is attributed to one of the powers this mythical creature bestows upon the magician.

Crowley changed these attributions, taken initially from Lévi, multiple times during his life and through his writings. Finally, in *Magick Without Tears* – toward the end of his life – he gives them as such:

- To will = Lion
- To dare = Eagle
- To know = Man
- To keep silence = Bull

The final power, 'To go', is attributed to the symbol of the Ankh. He states that 'To go' is the very meaning of the name God, of which the Ankh is a perfect symbol.

THE GREATER RITUAL OF THE PENTAGRAM

The **Greater Ritual of the Pentagram** (GRP) is a sort of higher-frequency, more elaborated version of the **Lesser Ritual of the Pentagram**. You will be already familiar with its magical effects and symbolism by now. However, adding the fifth element into the equation finally completes the circle.

Once you have fully integrated the lessons of the elements from the previous chapter, you will only keep this version in your magical arsenal when invoking or banishing a specific element is needed. For example, in *Liber O vel Manus et Sagittae* Crowley skips the lesser elemental pentagrams, making the point that Earth is made by the other three elements and represents their lower vibration. So he only uses the LBRP (banishing of Earth) and the GRP (both forms for the remaining elements).

I decided to go a bit slower, and I think the foundation of your magical pyramid will be much stronger because of it.

The ritual is as follows:

1. Perform the Qabalistic cross.
2. Go to the east. Make the invoking pentagram for active spirit and visualize it in white light. Vibrate the name EHEIEH while giving the sign of the rending of the veil.

THE SIGN OF THE RENDING OF THE VEIL

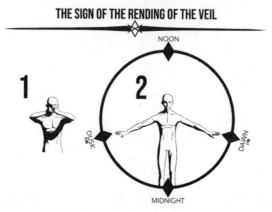

3. Make the invoking pentagram of Air, visualized in yellow light. Vibrate YHVH. Give the sign of Air, also known as the sign of the God Shu.

SIGN OF AIR

THE GOD SHU HOLDING THE SKY

4.   Trace the circle clockwise to the south. Make the invoking pentagram for active spirit. Visualize it in white light. Vibrate the name EHEIEH while giving the sign of the rending of the veil.

5.   Make the invoking pentagram of Fire, visualized in red light. Vibrate ELOHIM. Give the sign of Thoum-Aesh-Neith.

SIGN OF FIRE

THE GODDESS THOUM-AESH-NEITH

6.   Trace the circle clockwise to the west. Make the invoking pentagram for passive spirit visualized in white light. Vibrate AGLA. Give the sign of the closing of the veil.

THE SIGN OF THE CLOSING OF THE VEIL

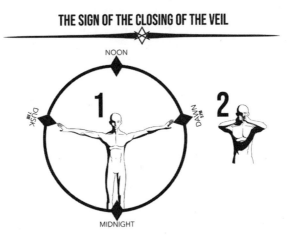

7.   Make the invoking pentagram of Water, visualized in blue light. Vibrate EL. Give the sign of Water, also known as the sign of the Goddess Auramoth.

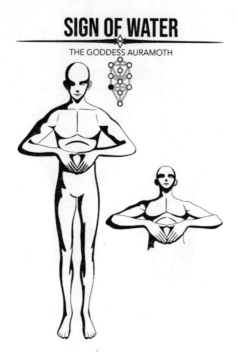

SIGN OF WATER
THE GODDESS AURAMOTH

8.   Trace the circle clockwise to the north. Make the invoking pentagram for passive spirit visualized in white light. Vibrate AGLA. Give the sign of the closing of the veil.

9.   Make the invoking pentagram of Earth, visualized in green light. Vibrate ADONAI. Give the sign of Earth, also known as the sign of the God Set fighting.

SIGN OF EARTH

THE GOD SET FIGHTING

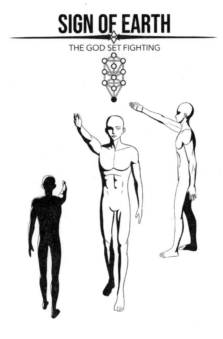

10. Complete tracing the circle clockwise to the east.
11. Return to the centre and perform the Qabalistic cross.

To perform the banishing version of the above, simply substitute banishing forms for all pentagrams, as seen in the previous chapter.

An additional pentagram is drawn at the four stations: the pentagrams of active and passive spirit. These are respectively given before the Air and Fire and Earth and Water quarters and should be visualized in white light. The divine name EHEIEH is used with the active spirit pentagrams, AGLA with passive spirit.

These spirit pentagrams effectively take the role of the angel invocations in the lesser ritual to underline that you are now closer to fully awakening in you the fifth element.

The new signs in each quarter can be understood as Western mudras. They are gestures and movements intended to signify and symbolize some aspect of spiritual truth. They represent one

grade of Outer College of the A∴A∴, and they take their names
– once again – from Egyptian gods.

Their presence in the ritual indicates the magician's mastery
over the elemental chaos. Therefore, their performance should
be approached with both intention and attention.

WHAT ABOUT THE SUPREME RITUAL OF THE PENTAGRAM THEN?

The supreme ritual of the pentagram and the hexagram are
later additions to the original Hermetic Order of the Golden
Dawn material found in the books of Israel Regardie.

While it's unclear whether these were Regardie's attempts
at creating new rituals, I have decided not to put them in the
essential arsenal of practices I am presenting here.

Remember: effectively, these rituals are 'old tech'. We need
it the way we need electricity for our computers to work. But
nowadays, we do use computers, not antiquated calculators.

THE LESSER RITUAL OF THE HEXAGRAM & THE FORMULA OF LVX

It's time we start looking at the next level of magical
consciousness expansion: the hexagram rituals.

Let's move the game forward and start exploring what
happens when one has ideally worked with the elements enough
to reach this first level of balance.

As with the pentagrams, we will start with the lesser version.
By now, it should be clear that 'lesser' does not mean 'lame',
and 'greater' does not mean 'awesome' in the parlance of

the magical system we are studying. The former indicates preparatory or generic, as the lesser rituals are performed to prepare your magical environment for any type of ritual. The latter, on the other hand, signifies particular, and as such, the greater rites come after the lesser rituals in order to attune the space – internal and external – to the proper element, planet, or sign for your operation.

LESSER RITUAL OF THE HEXAGRAM

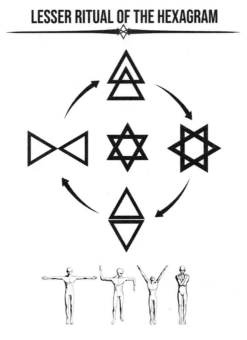

Here's the Lesser Ritual of the Hexagram, which must always be performed after the Lesser Ritual of the Pentagram:
Stand upright, feet together, left arm at the side, right arm across the body. Face east, and say in a clear voice:

I. N. R. I.
Yod. Nun. Resh. Yod.
Virgo, Isis, Mighty Mother.
Scorpio, Apophis, Destroyer.
Sol, Osiris, Slain and Risen.
Isis, Apophis, Osiris, IAO.

Then extend the arms in the form of a cross, and say:

The sign of Osiris Slain.

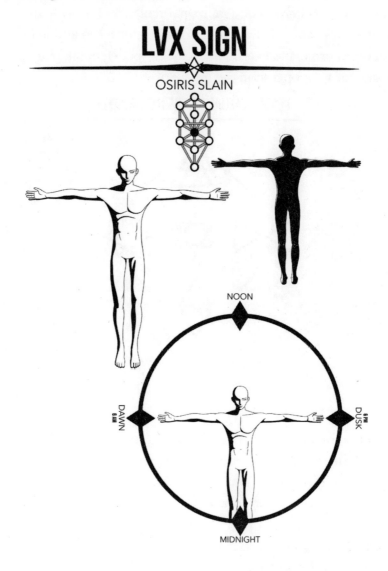

LVX SIGN

OSIRIS SLAIN

NOON

DAWN
6 AM

DUSK
6 PM

MIDNIGHT

Raise the right arm to point upwards, keeping the elbow square, and lower the left arm to point downwards, keeping the elbow square, while turning the head over the left shoulder, looking down so that the eyes follow the left forearm, and say:

The sign of the Mourning of Isis.

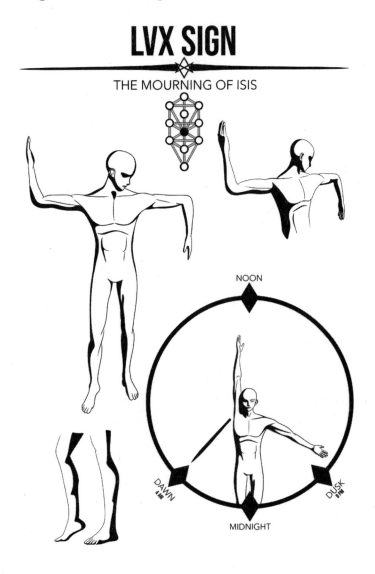

LVX SIGN

THE MOURNING OF ISIS

NOON

DAWN

DUSK

MIDNIGHT

Raise the arms at an angle of sixty degrees to each other above the head, which is thrown back, and say:

The sign of Apophis and Typhon.

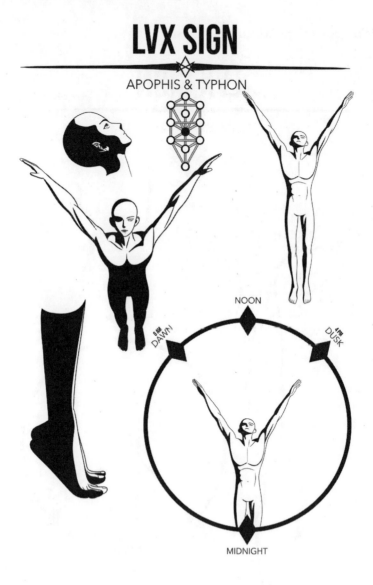

LVX SIGN

APOPHIS & TYPHON

NOON

DAWN 8AM

DUSK 4PM

MIDNIGHT

Cross the arms on the breast, bow the head, and say:

The sign of Osiris Risen

LVX SIGN

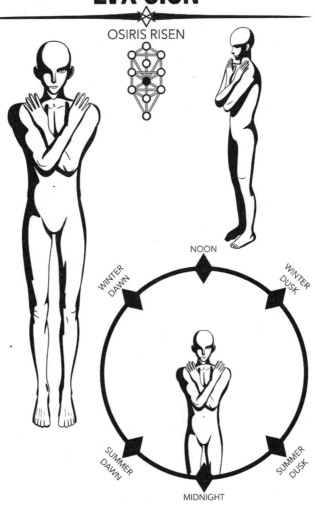

OSIRIS RISEN

NOON

WINTER DAWN

WINTER DUSK

SUMMER DAWN

SUMMER DUSK

MIDNIGHT

Repeat both signs of Osiris (Slain, then Risen), and then say:

LVX, Lux, the light of the cross.

Trace the hexagram of Fire in the east while vibrating ARARITA.[18]
Trace the hexagram of Earth in the south while vibrating ARARITA.
Trace the hexagram of Air in the west while vibrating ARARITA.
Trace the hexagram of Water in the north while vibrating ARARITA.

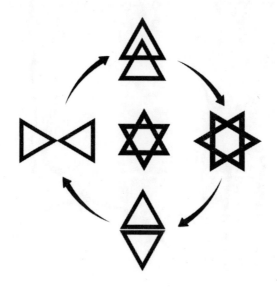

Repeat the signs of LVX as in the beginning.

The direction of the hexagrams must be reversed to banish the energy instead of invoking it.

When you start working with this ritual, you will probably notice that elemental directions are different. Earlier in the book, we discussed why: the hexagram is macrocosmic in nature and follows the zodiacal attributions of the elements rather than the terrestrial one.

---

[18] This word consists of the initials of a Hebrew sentence *Achad Rosh Achdoto Rosh Ichudo Teumrato Achad*, which means 'One is His Beginning: One is His Individuality: His Permutation is One'.

It's essential to notice that the hexagram symbolizes the sun, the great equalizing power in the solar system and the source of matter in the solar system. All matter results from the condensing of solar energy. This energy concentrates in stages, represented by the elements themselves, from Fire, to Air, Water, and finally solid matter, or Earth.

And this is why this ritual is so powerful. It allows you to access the solar power in all its manifestations and alchemically rewire your entire being on a physical (Earth), emotional (Water), mental (Air), and spiritual (Fire) level.

The new signs you learned are collectively called the **signs of LVX**. LVX is the Latin word for 'light', and in the Hermetic Order of the Golden Dawn, they were attributed to the grade of the adept – the one who has mastered the powers of the sphinx and reached Heliopolis.

This brief text essentially recalls the Osirian myth, in which Osiris is killed by his brother Set and revived by his wife Isis.

Set is not the same as Apophis or Typhon, despite the fact that they are frequently confused by modern practitioners. In Egyptian mythology, Apophis or Apep was the snake who lurked beneath the horizon each night, attempting to consume the sun as it went through the underworld.

The association of Apep with Set is especially hilarious because it was Set who defended Ra's bark from this enormous snake, therefore preventing the sun from being devoured every night. Set and Apep were, in reality, enemies. Typhon is a Greek god who, like Apep, represents chaos, which is why the two are merged in this sign. In the context of the Osirian myth, Apophis and Typhon allude to Osiris passing into the underworld symbolized by Apep – not the identity of his murderer.

Once you have finished giving the signs of LVX (also described as the **analysis of the keyword**), you begin in the east and move clockwise, tracing the hexagram of each element to the appropriate direction as you vibrate **ARARITA**.

This word essentially means **unity** and is one of the most fundamental magical formulae of Thelema.

The elemental hexagrams are made up of two triangles. Fire is represented by the upward-pointing triangle, while Water is represented by the downward-pointing triangle. As a result, Fire is Fire over Fire, Earth is Fire balanced with Water, Air is Fire over Water, and Water is Water over Fire. They also resemble their corresponding elemental weapons, which can be a helpful mnemonic. For example, Fire would be the wand, Earth the pantacle, Air the dagger, and Water the cup. Looking at the shapes closely, you can see how they line up.

A MAGICAL 'YMCA' DANCE?

In a time where we lost almost all the reverence for magick and mysticism (and sometimes it's not too bad a thing), those approaching this stage of these practices make a somewhat expected remark: are these mystical signs nothing but a weird magical 'YMCA' dance?

Well, it sure looks like it, doesn't it?

However, you should remember what I already told you before: these are, by all means, mudras. That is, shapes that synthesize complex concepts meant to invoke inside you as you make them.

The origin of the signs of LVX is likely lost at this stage, or maybe I haven't been able to find it beyond a reasonable doubt. But, quite simply, one could argue that since the concept of the astral light is so essential, these signs simply spell out the letters L V X in human shapes – and they do. Another possibility is that they are derived from the plethora of masonic modes of recognition since the Hermetic Order of the Golden Dawn derived directly from the masonic Societas

Rosicruciana In Anglia[19] and most of its members were also prominent Freemasons.

I was taught something different, however, and while researching and cross-checking my references for this book, I was able to source the origin of that teaching. It is from a somewhat obscure paper titled 'Concerning the True System of Astrological Divination', which was part of a lecture of the Hermetic Order of the Golden Dawn reserved for the **Theoreticus Adeptus Minor** sub-degree. This document was found in the collection of **Dr Carnegie Dickson** (Frater Fortes Fortuna Juvat), a member of the Stella Matutina.[20] It is fascinating since one notation states, 'Copied from SA's "Chief Adept's" Copy of May 1885. FFJ.' – SA being Sapere Aude, or **William Wynn Wescott**,[21] one of the founders of the Golden Dawn.

The following images might help you understand it all better:

---

[19] Societas Rosicruciana in Anglia (Rosicrucian Society of England, abbreviated to SRIA) is a Rosicrucian esoteric Christian order formed by Robert Wentworth Little in 1865. Members are confirmed from the ranks of subscribing Master Masons of a Grand Lodge in amity with United Grand Lodge of England. (*Wikipedia*) (Of all the orders I became a member of, SRIA is the only one that formally requested me to pretend my initiation never happened once they recognized me as a 'prominent Thelemite'. But this is a story for another time…)

[20] The Stella Matutina (Morning Star) was an initiatory magical order dedicated to the dissemination of the traditional teachings of the earlier Hermetic Order of the Golden Dawn. The Stella Matutina was one of several daughter organizations into which the Hermetic Order of the Golden Dawn fragmented, including the Alpha et Omega led by John William Brodie-Innes and Macgregor Mathers, the Isis-Urania Temple led by A E Waite, and others. (*Wikipedia*)

[21] William Wynn Westcott (17 December 1848–30 July 1925) was a coroner, ceremonial magician, theosophist, and Freemason born in Leamington, Warwickshire, England. He was a Supreme Magus of the SRIA and went on to co-found the Golden Dawn. (*Wikipedia*)

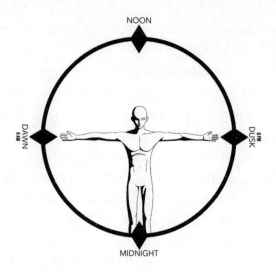

THE SIGN OF OSIRIS SLAIN

It represents the equinoctial forces.

EQUINOXES: Length of day and night equal.

THE SIGN OF THE MOURNING OF ISIS

This is the power of light at its peak, hence the space between the hands represents the sun's semi-arc during the summer solstice. She thus recalls it as the affirmation of the life force of Osiris.

SUMMER SOLSTICE: Day length greatest, night length least.

THE SIGN OF TYPHON AND APOPHIS

At the winter solstice, the gap between the hands above the head will represent the reduced extent of the sun's total area. It symbolizes the dominance of darkness over light.

WINTER SOLSTICE: Length of night greatest, day least.

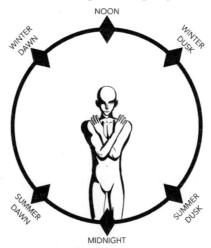

THE SIGN OF OSIRIS RISEN

The synthetical extent of the vibration between the solstice's maximum light and the equinox. It affirms that the governance of these forces may be found in the self depending on the higher illumination.

THE WHOLE YEAR: All variations of day and night.

A MASONIC DETOUR

'Erected to God and dedicated to Holy Saints John' is a phrase familiar to all Freemasons. Every time I heard this while sitting in lodge, I wondered what the symbolism of St John the Baptist and St John the Evangelist was in Freemasonry. They are often simply described as patron saints of the brotherhood and accepted as such by Christian and non-Christian Freemasons alike.

The Gospel of Luke (1:36, 56–57) states that John was born about six months before Jesus, therefore the feast of John the Baptist was fixed on 24 June, six months before Christmas Eve. The feast day of 24 June is celebrated with water being used in the ceremony. The festival coincides obviously with the entrance of Cancer, the cardinal sign of the Water element, and on the summer solstice when the path of the sun in the sky is farthest north in the northern hemisphere, which has the longest day and shortest night.

Conversely, the feast of St John the Evangelist is celebrated on 27 December, a few days after the sun enters Capricorn, the cardinal sign of Earth. Apostle John was a historical figure, one of the pillars of the Jerusalem church after the death of Jesus. He was one of Christ's original 12 apostles and is thought to be the only one to have lived into old age, retiring to the island of Patmos to endure a visionary ordeal that gave us the *Book of Revelation*. More commonly known as *The Apocalypse*, this book is fundamental to Thelema due to the gnosis received through the scrying of the Enochian aethyrs that Crowley codified in *The Vision and the Voice*. It's there that we find Therion and, more importantly, Babalon.

From the interlocked hexagram, which is also represented by the masonic square and compass, St John the Baptist represents the inverted pyramid pointing downward, the elemental Water, and symbolizes emotional love ruled by the moon. St John the

Evangelist, designated as the pyramid pointing up, symbolizes the elemental Fire that is the drive and will of action. When placed together, they represent the perfect balance of darkness and light, life and death, passion and constraint, will and emotion, summer and winter, Cancer and Capricorn.

Polarities and Duality. We heard that before.

A symbol special to Freemasonry is the circle with a point in the centre between two parallel tangent lines. The two St Johns are thought to be represented by these tangents. The circle depicts the yearly cycle of the sun through the zodiac, with the point representing the sun and the circle representing the zodiac. And now, we can also realize where the astronomical and alchemical symbol for the sun comes from.

The two parallel lines are tangents to the circle at the Cancer and Capricorn solstitial points. They mark the upper and lower limits of the sun's ascension and fall across the ecliptic plane. Because these two tangent points represent the two solstices, these two gates represent the two St Johns.

> The galaxy crosses the zodiac in two opposite points, Cancer and Capricorn, the tropical points in the sun's course ordinarily called the gates of the sun. The Milky Way crossed at the signs of Cancer and Capricorn.

This quotation by **Macrobius** alludes to the symbolism referred to as the masonic symbol of the sun and the two tangent lines. Those are, in the macroscopic sense, the two gates of the sun.

Above: The masonic Saints, John the Baptist and John the Evangelist, guarding the 'gates of the sun'

Albert Pike,[22] in his seminal masonic magnum opus, *Morals and Dogma*, states:

> Through these gates souls were supposed to descend to Earth and reascend to Heaven. One, was styled the Gate of Men, and the other, the Gate of the Gods. Cancer was the former, because souls descended by it to the Earth. Capricorn the latter, because by it they reascended to their seats of immortality and became gods.
>
> Thus the secret science and mysterious emblems of initiation were connected with the heavens, the spheres and the constellations, and this connection must be studied by

---

[22] Albert Pike (December 29, 1809–April 2, 1891) was an American author, poet, orator, editor, lawyer, jurist, and Confederate general who served as an associate justice of the Arkansas Supreme Court in exile from 1864 to 1865. A prominent member of the Freemasons, Pike served as the Sovereign Grand Commander of the Supreme Council, Scottish Rite (Southern Jurisdiction, USA) from 1859 to 1889. (*Wikipedia*)

whomsoever would understand the ancient mind and be enabled to interpret the allegories and explore the meaning of the symbols.[23]

Consider once again the message behind the practice of the solar adorations in light of what we just discussed. In the new aeon, one does not live 'in the son' any longer but perpetually 'in the sun'.

BEYOND THE SUN:
THE GREATER RITUAL OF THE HEXAGRAM
& THE PLANETARY INFLUENCES

Unlike the Lesser Ritual of the Hexagram, Crowley does not provide step-by-step instruction for the Greater Ritual of the Hexagram. However, he makes it clear that this ritual is needed to invoke or banish the zodiacal and planetary influences − moving beyond the sun into the stars themselves.

These are all the instructions he left us:

- Only use the hexagram of Earth.
- Trace the astrological sigil of the planet in the centre of your hexagram. (For the zodiac, use the hexagram of the planet which rules the sign you require; but draw the astrological sigil of the sign.)
- Then use a conjuration which includes the formula ARARITA first, and following with the name of the God corresponding to the planet or sign you are dealing with.

The following images should help you untangle this puzzle:

---

[23] From his commentary on the 25th degree or 'Knight of the Brazen Serpent'.

COLOUR
BLACK
GODNAME
YHVH ELOHIM

COLOUR
BLUE
GODNAME
EL

COLOUR
SCARLET RED
GODNAME
ELOHIM GIBOR

COLOUR
GOLD
GODNAME
YHVH ELOAH
V'DAATH

COLOUR
EMERALD GREEN
GODNAME
YHVH
TZABAOTH

COLOUR
ORANGE
GODNAME
ELOHIM
TZABAOTH

COLOUR
VIOLET
GODNAME
SHADDAI
EL CHAI

Above and opposite: The planetary and zodiacal hexagrams

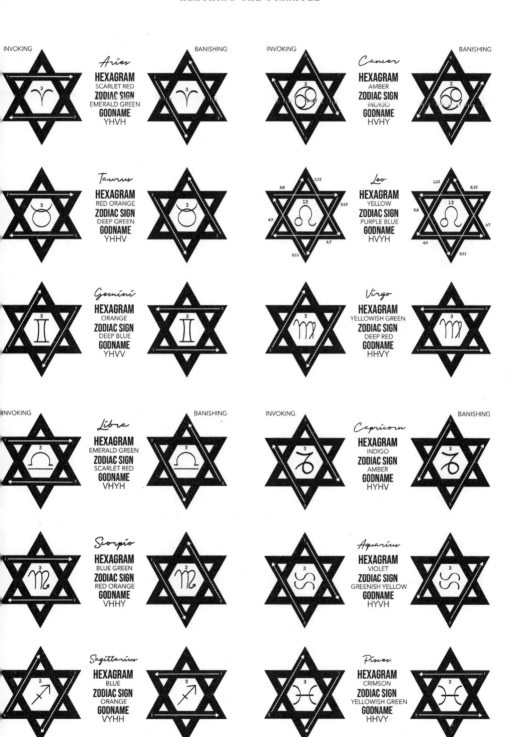

The simplest way to proceed is to use the same format as the Lesser Ritual of the Hexagram, except for the different figures drawn. The conjurations specified by Crowley are then simple vibrations of the magical formula ARARITA and the name of the god corresponding to the planet or sign.

Alternatively, you can go for a more sophisticated approach. The conjurations, in this case, are more elaborate invocations, and the ritual must be carefully tailored to the specific occasion and purpose.

For example, to invoke Jupiter, you would face the direction of Jupiter at the place and hour appointed and sound a battery of four knocks (four being the number of Jupiter). Then you would recite an ARARITA invocation (derived in this case from *Liber DCCCXIII*):

> O my God! One is Thy Beginning! One is Thy spirit, and Thy Permutation One! Thou has appeared unto me as a jocund and ruddy God, full of Majesty, a King, a Father in his prime. Thou didst bear the sceptre of the Universe, crowned with the Wheel of the Spirit. ARARITA!

Having drawn the proper hexagram, you would proceed to an invocation of Jupiter. This example is modified slightly from Thomas Taylor's translation of the Orphic Hymn to *Jove, as the Author of Lightning*:

> Come, O JOVE, on Thee I call! JOVE! JOVE!
> I call the mighty, holy splendid light,
> Aerial, dreadful-sounding, fiery-bright;
> Flaming, aerial-light, with angry voice,
> Lightning thro' lucid clouds with horrid noise.
> Untam'd, to whom resentments dire belong,
> Pure, holy pow'r all-parent, great and strong:
> Come, and benevolent these rites attend,
> And aid my will to realize its end.

As you can see, you have a lot of work ahead of you in carefully crafting each of the seven rituals. Fun times! Doing so, however, will also be your first attempt at creating your own magick – which is the point of all this training.

A HIGHER FREQUENCY

Let's stop and recap all that we have learned so far. The pentagrams represent the plane of the terrestrial elements. The hexagrams represent that of the planets, centred in the sun, ultimately a symbol of the Holy Guardian Angel and spirit.

In working with these planetary energies, you will quickly discover that they represent a higher level of divine power and consciousness. If the elementals are below the magical coherence level of the magician's ego-consciousness, the planetary influences are likewise above that level.

This higher frequency can result in magick that, if not precisely dangerous, is at least more difficult. Mood swings, emotional problems, and even obsession could manifest if you rush into practices you aren't ready for. A thorough and complete grounding in more general magical work is one of the best means of avoiding these difficulties. If something feels odd, STOP and banish it.

DAILY PRACTICE (DURATION: 2 MONTHS)

✪ Perform the Greater Ritual of the Pentagram.

✪ Keep recording your insights on the elements inside and in the space around you in your magical diary.

✪ After two weeks, switch to performing the Lesser Ritual of the Hexagram. As mentioned, this ritual is always preceded by the LBRP, so be aware of the time needed – don't rush things!

✪ Make notes of the following:

   ✶ Increase of vitality (solar influence on Earth)

   ✶ A greater feeling of unity and empathy with the cosmos (solar influence on Water)

   ✶ Increase in intuition (solar influence on Air)

   ✶ First glimpses of the vision of the angel (solar influence on Fire)

✪ After a month, add the Greater Ritual of the Hexagram to your routines. Use it to invoke each planetary influence on the appropriate day of the week.

✪ Remember to keep yourself in check: these higher-frequency rituals can be very impactful. If you notice unexpected mood swings, take a break from any practice for at least a few days.

THIS IS WHERE THELEMA STARTS

CHAPTER 6

THIS IS WHERE THELEMA STARTS

And here we are, at long last … I bet you must be surprised that a book whose subtitle is *Thelemic Magick for Modern Times* only starts discussing Thelema almost at its end. By now, I am also sure you must have understood why. Without first working through the old aeonic formula of LVX and its foundation in the elements, we simply cannot fully engage with the magick of the new aeon.

A SHORT INTRODUCTION TO AEONICS

Crowley theorized that the history of humanity can be divided into a series of aeons. Each was accompanied by its own forms of magical and religious expression. So as time went on, newer and better ways to unlock our full potential were made available.

You can think of it as purchasing a new model of your favourite brand of phone or computer, as well as installing on it a new operating system. The first is independent of you: you must wait for that model to become available. The second, however, is entirely your choice: you can, in fact, keep using the old operating system if you so wish. Just don't expect it to run as efficiently as the latest, and there might be feats you simply cannot do without the upgrade.

The concept of the magical formula (which we will discuss in more detail later on) is crucial for this aeonics theory. Each aeon brings a new formula: those are the new 'operating systems' I just mentioned.

This is why embracing Thelema does matter. The formula of Thelema allows humanity to embrace its spiritual evolution faster and better. By building the magical pyramid, you are now at the stage where you can start understanding the next step.

However, you must become familiar with a few new concepts first. Therefore, we will start with a panorama of the aeons so far.

THE AEON OF ISIS

The earliest of them was the aeon of the mother, which, according to Crowley, occurred throughout prehistory and saw humanity worshipping a great goddess, portrayed by the ancient Egyptian divinity Isis.

The aeon of Isis was maternal, with the female aspect of the godhead adored as a result of a primarily matriarchal culture and the belief that Mother Earth nursed, clothed, and housed humanity while it was still in its womb. It was distinguished by its devotion to the mother and nature.

THE AEON OF OSIRIS

This was followed by the aeon of the father, which Crowley corresponds to the classical and medieval centuries. This was when humanity worshipped a singular male god and was dominated by patriarchal values.

The aeon of Osiris is dominated by the paternal principle, self-sacrifice and submission to the almighty father in Heaven. This is very much the time of Judaism, Christianity, and Islam, and the fact our world seems very much steeped into these principles even now, almost 120 years after Crowley's reception of *Liber AL vel Legis*, should make us pause for a moment and consider the historical validity of aeonics. More on this further on.

In *The Heart of the Master*, Crowley tells us that this aeon is centred on the formula of Osiris, whose word is IAO – the same we met while studying and practising the hexagram rituals. Another critical point was considering humanity as wholly subject to death and his victory dependent upon resurrection. This was shown by the sun as slain and reborn every day and every year; the study and practice of *Liber Resh vel Helios* taught us that, in the current aeon, this perspective has now changed completely.

THE AEON OF HORUS

The third (and current) aeon is the aeon of the child and is symbolized by Horus. In it, humanity shall enter a time of self-realization and self-actualization. Again, individuality and finding one's True Will are the dominant aspects; its formula is that of growth both in consciousness and love.

There have been some interesting historical precedents that alluded to the aeon of Horus. The most notable must be the mention of the Abbey of Thélème in *Gargantua and Pantagruel* by **François Rabelais**, a connected series of books that tell the story of two giants – a father (Gargantua) and his son (Pantagruel) and their adventures – written in an amusing, extravagant, and satirical vein. Rabelais was a Christian monk, and his philosophy is much more Stoic than it is Thelemic. Still, Crowley was inspired by his works and went on to establish his own Abbey of Thelema in Cefalú, Italy, in the early 1920s. In 1926, he started writing *The Antecedents of Thelema* to showcase the philosophical connections with Rabelais' ideas, but the book would remain incomplete.

Another possible precursor was **Sir Francis Dashwood**, who adopted some of the ideas of Rabelais and invoked the same rule as 'Do what thou wilt' in French (*fais ce que tu voudras*) when he founded a group called the 'Monks of Medmenham' (better known as 'The Hellfire Club'). In reality, we know awfully little of Dashwood's beliefs and practices.

Something to bear in mind is that Horus is a composite deity. By Horus, we really refer to Heru-Ra-Ha, who is in turn made of its active aspect (Ra-Hoor-Khuit, the voice of the third chapter of *Liber AL vel Legis*) and passive aspect (Hoor-Paar-Kraat, more commonly referred to by the Greek rendering *Harpocrates*). More on this later.

If you are confused … strap in, as it will be a bumpy ride from now on!

FUTURE AEONS

We find traces of the next aeon already in *Liber AL vel Legis* (III.34), and even more so through Crowley's words directly. In *The Confessions*, we learn that Horus will be, in his turn, succeeded by Thmaist, the 'double-wanded one', who shall bring the candidates to complete initiation.

Crowley admitted he knew very little about this character, other than her name was 'justice' – which is why some Thelemites think the aeon of Ma'at will replace the current one.

According to Charles Stansfeld Jones (aka Frater Achad), one of Crowley's early disciples, the aeon of Ma'at has already begun or overlaps the current aeon of Horus. These theories were expanded upon by other adepts, such as **Kenneth Grant** and **Nema Andahadna** – the latter being the founder of a post-Thelemic system called 'Maat magick'.

WHAT IF IT'S ALL MADE UP?

In writing about the revelations of the new aeon, Crowley always presented these things as absolute facts. But, of course, he could do it mainly because he was writing in a time before modern science truly took hold and when academic scrutiny wasn't as rigorous as it is today.

For instance, in *The Book of the Thoth*, he states that 'the magical doctrine of the succession of the aeons is connected with the precession of the zodiac.' The aeon of Isis is connected to the signs of Aries and Libra. The aeon of Osiris referred to Pisces and Virgo. And finally, the aeon of Horus is linked to Aquarius and Leo.

Unfortunately for him, the aeons of Isis, Osiris and Horus do not easily conform to astronomers' recent calculations or astrologers' disputed issues. And so it becomes clear that the theory of aeonics must once again be taken not as a scientific fact. Instead, it is a model we can work with while trying to map what's likely beyond the scope of language and rationality: the magical and mystical experience as a whole.

It's also important to understand that aeons do overlap. Stop for a second, and consider that we are trying to force these larger-than-human concepts into something we can make sense of. Deities, if they do exist, are not bound to our physical bodies or our notions of space and time. Once you've accepted this, you can see how we can use the magick of Horus while still living in a world that seems very much rooted in the laws of Osiris, and while the promise of Ma'at and the nurturing nature of Isis can be found among those able to channel those lessons.

THE WHO'S WHO OF THELEMIC THEOLOGY

By now, you must be asking yourself if Thelema is a religion since we spoke of vast aggregates of consciousness, or deities. I remarked just above that we cannot be sure if these deities exist, and I am going to take a moment here to remind you of the intimation from *Liber O* that we encountered at the beginning of our journey.

Once again: it's immaterial whether these deities exist or not. From our perspective, that of the magician, we know that if we use rituals that involve them, results will follow. I am well aware that this might seem like a reductivist approach that flies in the face of every single philosopher out there. But going too deep into the philosophical implications of Thelema is far beyond the scope of this book.

In *Magick Without Tears*, Crowley writes:

> To sum up, our system is a religion just so far as a religion means
> an enthusiastic putting-together of a series of doctrines, no one
> of which must in any way clash with Science or Magick. Call it
> a new religion, then, if it so please your Gracious Majesty; but I
> confess that I fail to see what you will have gained by so doing,
> and I feel bound to add that you might easily cause a great deal
> of misunderstanding, and work a rather stupid kind of mischief.

That said, I must make my own position clear: for me, the 'gods' of Thelema are not ancient Egyptian at all; they are Egyptoid at best. Their meaning and nature are not necessarily related to their closest historical namesakes.

Thelema is, therefore, not a revival of Egyptian religion in any tangible way, and the study of Egyptology gives no real insight into them as they are not the same. In fact, confusing them for historical gods and conflating their stories with old mythologies may complicate and dilute the new Thelemic meanings.

That said, studying other mythologies and systems (such as philosophy or psychology) is just as helpful as studying ancient Egyptian religion as we know it, and the latter is not inherently more true or Thelemic. In fact, Thelema bears innumerably more similarities to various forms of Christianity than anything resembling ancient Egyptian religion.

I write this being absolutely aware that other Thelemites will disagree with me, some vehemently too. But, if you intend to become a Thelemite yourself – and if you are reading these words, there is a good chance that's your intention – you must accept that if you ask ten Thelemites one question, you will likely receive 111 different answers. It's part and parcel of interacting with a system of theology and philosophy still in its infancy. But, I argue it's also one of its most exciting parts.

THE ACTORS ON THE STELE OF REVEALING

The stele of Ankh-f-n-Khonsu is a painted wooden offering stele that was discovered in 1858 by François Auguste Ferdinand Mariette at the mortuary temple of the 18th Dynasty Pharaoh Hatshepsut (one of the few historically confirmed female pharaohs), located at Dayr al-Bahri.

Above: The Stele of Revealing

It was this stele that Rose Kelly, the first of Crowley's wives (and the first of his scarlet women with the name 'Ouarda the Seer'), indicated as the source of the communication she was receiving from 'somewhere else' that would lead to the inauguration of the new aeon of the child. On their honeymoon in Cairo, Rose would state that 'the god Horus' was angry at Crowley for ignoring him. Surprised by his wife's strange accuracy when questioned on the characteristics of this 'god', especially since she had never shown any interest in religion or spirituality thus far, Crowley took her to the Egyptian Museum. Furthering his surprise, she pointed at the stele when asked to 'find Horus'.

The stele depicts four figures: the human figure is Ankh-f-n-Khonsu himself, a priest of the deity Mentu. He is making sacrifices to the falcon-headed god Ra-Harakhty ('Ra-Horus of the two horizons'), a throne-seated syncretic manifestation of the gods Ra and Horus. Behind Re-Harakhty is the emblem of the west, the land of the dead. Nut, the sky goddess who reaches from horizon to horizon, is depicted above the figurines. Horus of Behdet, the winged solar disk, is just underneath her.

Recognizing the tremendous value of the message received, Crowley renamed it the **Stele of Revealing** and requested the museum's curator to arrange a translation of the hieroglyphs. We can infer that somehow the translators missed something here or there, as Crowley would go on to name the three deities **Nuit**, **Hadit** and **Ra-Hoor-Khuit**. These are the three voices of *The Book of the Law* chapters. Let's get to know them a little better.

NUIT & HADIT

NUIT

Nuit is the French word for 'night'. So her name is entirely consistent with the nature of the goddess who describes herself as 'Infinite Space, and the Infinite Stars thereof'. Stop for a moment here, and look at how these words are capitalized in the text of *Liber AL*. Therein, you will already find an essential hint on the true nature of her: the initiatrix of the old mysteries, Isis.

As the circumference, she is a circle, resembling the number zero, symbol of the vulva. Though she is **The All**, she resists being called **The One**: the **whole** of existence cannot be named 'one'. When there is no differentiation of substance, zero ('nothing') is the better representation. In a closed system (such as the universe), 'all' is the same as 'nothing': both indicate that no subset is distinguished from the whole.

Once we distinguish a single point within the whole, the result is rightly called *two* things: self and other, the differentiated point of view and the rest of creation. When the boundaries between them dissolve (when a point of view 'dies' in the body of the infinite, surrendering its distinction), *two* again become *none*.

She says: 'With the God & the Adorer I am nothing … I am Heaven, and there is no other God than me, and my lord Hadit.' The second 'God' is singular: note the word 'and'. The 'only God' is **the two of them together.** She is 'nothing' **with** Hadit. As perfect complements, their sum is 0.

Regarding worship, Nuit's servants are 'few & secret', but others are also called to her worship. We are to invoke her under her stars and celebrate 'A feast every night unto Nu, and the pleasure of uttermost delight!' Her incense is of resinous woods and gums, 'and there is no blood therein'. She demands nothing in sacrifice. Her number, colour, and symbols are given in her book.

She asks us to sing to her 'the rapturous love-song', burn incense, wear jewels in her honour, and drink to her.

A long passage describing a particular way to worship her (and promising rewards) is given in *Liber AL* I.61–63. Also, one extraordinary verse lays out an entire curriculum of spiritual attainment in three ethical directives: 'Obey my prophet! follow out the ordeals of my knowledge! seek me only! Then the joys of my love will redeem ye from all pain.' In stark difference from

other religions, her rewards are not withheld until some vague
time after death.

Thelema's core aphorisms appear in chapter I. Nuit says
'Sin is Restriction', to be understood as denying one's true
nature. She instructs us to unite freely in love; live lives of joy,
certainty, and unutterable peace, tolerant of differences; adore
the stellar light within us; and uplift ourselves, rousing our 'coiled
splendour' unto her love.

HADIT

Hadit is an entirely new name appearing in *The Book of the Law*
– or, more precisely, in the events of spring 1904 leading to the
text's reception. In the Cairo Museum, the Crowleys discovered a
funeral stele depicting all the main characters that would appear
in the book. Crowley had the hieroglyphs translated and then
paraphrased the text into poetry. During the book's dictation,
Aiwass instructed him to insert part of that poetry into the book.

The museum staff transcribed a name now known to be
Behdety as Hudit. Crowley wrote this as Hadit in his poetic
paraphrase. Once registered in the book, the name was
canonical. That's because the book tells us that its text is not to
be modified in any way. So whatever ancient Egyptians called
this god, its name in *Liber AL vel Legis* is Hadit.

Hadit resembles the name Hades, meaning 'unseen'. Hades–
Hadit is the 'hidden one', buried in our secret centre. The Hadit
chapter is 'the secret that hath not yet been revealed'. He says he
shall never be truly known. Even his servants are 'masked ones',
their true natures veiled.

Some Thelemites have noticed a similarity between this name
and the Latin verb *vadit,* meaning 'he goes'; essential to Hadit's
nature is that **he goes.**

Symbolized by the centre point of a circle or sphere, Had is
the sperm fertilizing a **self-gestating ovum-universe** that
grows into a new child-universe. As the life seed deep in each

of us, concentrating life's fires, Hadit personifies our individual points of view.

Yet this single point at the centre of the universe is not stationary: it is in motion, even as each person's point of view is in motion, witnessing reality through a shifting panorama of a unique experience. The nature of experience is to be inevitably individual. Looking at the same object from different points in space always produces a distinct impression.

As Nuit's complement and mate, Hadit always desires intimate union with her. The deep passion of our lives is always to mate with Nuit; however, we encounter her to experience each circumstance or event as intimately as possible. Passing *casually* through life experience is infidelity to our mate and to ourselves.

As god of life and aliveness, Hadit is called 'the worshipper'. This summons us to experience life in a state of wonder. Nuit calls Hadit the universe's centre, heart, and voice ('tongue'), then beckons us **to be that**.

As a seed of identity, Hadit is existentially isolated, alone, abiding in innocence at our centre, forming and dissolving our reality (both the magician and the exorcist). He is the silence that has been worshipped by all who have worshipped the god of silence. In this, we see echoes of the passive aspect of Horus, Hoor-Paar-Kraat: as I told you above, it was going to get more confusing, and this is because you must learn to avoid thinking in strict binaries and 'neat little boxes' when thinking of these vast aggregates of consciousness we call 'deities'.

In Qabalistic terms, Hadit is best represented by the Hebrew letter *yod*, which corresponds on the Tree of Life both to Kether (the unextended inmost point of light, the essence of being) and Chokhmah (the paternal will or going).

Despite Hadit's disdain for those who worship him (since he is the one in us who worships), he still advises on how to do it best. This involves living a full, impassioned, and deeply satisfying life in which we 'exceed by delicacy', refining our rapture and bringing subtlety to our joy. He tells us to celebrate 'A feast every day in your hearts in the joy of my rapture!' He encourages intoxication. He dismisses the thought that we could be damned for enjoyment.

Like Nuit, he gives a curriculum of spiritual attainment in three directives of ethical conduct: 'But remember, o chosen one, to be me; to follow the love of Nu in the star-lit heaven; to look forth upon men, to tell them this glad word.' (Nu is Nuit.)

Hadit gives further ethical instructions throughout chapter II. All deal with vitality and enthusiasm in life; the cessation of fear, sorrow, smallness, and other 'folly against self', and the enhancement of joy through strength and skill.

RA-HOOR-KHUIT

In the Egyptian pantheon, many permutations of Ra (a sun-god) and Horus/Heru/Hoor (a god of war) exist. However, Ra-Hoor-Khuit is explicitly Ra-Hoor as a *khu*.

Khu is an ancient Egyptian term for the incarnating aspect of a person, the soul that leaves the body at death and travels the Egyptian bardo still bearing the identity it knew on Earth. Traditional characteristics and powers of the *khu* are those of a magician's mature body of light, which we discussed at length in the book's opening chapters.

Therefore, Ra-Hoor-Khuit is a particular solar-martial fusion of Ra and Hoor forged into the inner aspect of a human soul. A god created in humanity's image, **divinity bridging to humanity**, accessible by us in the image of our inner solar–stellar nature.

RA HOOR KHU T

In contrast to Nuit and Hadit, Ra-Hoor-Khuit is explicitly **the visible object of worship**. This might be his most important characteristic.

He is emphatically a warrior god. However, ongoing discussions in Thelemic communities debate exactly what the warrior passages in *Liber AL* mean. While some take them as a direct call to arms and battle, I suggest a more nuanced approach:

- Our greatest battles are within ourselves. In the domain of self-mastery, life (especially the Great Work of spiritual unfolding) is a campaign of self-conquest.
- Life is an ongoing struggle. It constantly challenges us to be better – to become stronger, more precise, more insightful, more connected, and more aware – to harvest and refine our distinctive greatness. Just as the best wine comes from grapes that have to fight through hard soil and harsh conditions, human excellence arises from the struggle of emerging as ourselves through the fires of the ordeal. This is an inner battle. Extreme conditions may mirror the internal hardship or not, depending on our choices.
- Predictably, human society's resistance to the new Thelemic worldview has stirred inevitable conflict during this transition since 1904. This conflict results from collective inertia, restriction, and weakness – traits *The Book of the Law* disparages. The existence or need for war is evidence of where we have fallen short thus far.

As the 'visible object of worship', reflecting our own solar-stellar nature to us, Ra-Hoor-Khuit is also called the 'lord initiating', the hierophant ('revealer of the mysteries', or inner teacher) of the new aeon.

Technically, the lord of the aeon appears to be a different form of the Ra-Horus amalgam, **Heru-Ra-Ha** – Horus and Ra united with Ha, a term implying spirit and the final word of *The Book of the Law*. Heru-Ra-Ha is a twin god, manifesting in **stirring** and **stilling** aspects, the 'twin warriors' Ra-Hoor-Khuit and Hoor-Paar-Kraat.

Liber AL provides more details on the worship of Ra-Hoor-Khuit than of either Nuit or Hadit. However, here are relevant instructions on worship from chapter III:

- First of all, it tells us to give him reverence, and to rejoice in all the ordeals that have brought us to him, and to Thelema (*AL* III:62).
- He makes no secret that Thelema's true nature is found not so much in presenting the other cheek, but in enjoying conflict (*AL* III:9).
- Fire and blood, swords and spears are all sacred to him. Again, a reference to the fact that the Thelemite should not be meek and cowardly, but strong and proud. He also tells us that in the new aeon, the secret mysteries of the divine feminine are at its centre (*AL* III:11). Although the first impression often drawn is that this means 'spill blood for me, kill for me', *Liber AL* doesn't specify this. Blood flows monthly in the menses and moment-by-moment in our veins. Let this pumping of our blood and every pulse of our hearts be dedicated to Ra-Hoor-Khuit!
- Concerning his altar, he specifies that it should be made of open brass work, and there you should burn fine incenses related to silver and gold. This might also be a reference to secret sexual rites (*AL* III:30).
- This altar should be set up in the east of your temple, and its form much like that of the traditional Horus of Egypt. Mine is a hawk wearing the crown of Upper and Lower Egypt. He also states that there should be images of every other god, spirit, or entity you work with around him (*AL* III:21). This verse portrays Ra-Hoor-Khuit as the central mystery behind all gods.

He provides a formula for incense made of meal and honey and thick leavings of red wine, to which you are meant to add oil of Abramelin and olive oil. Unlike the incense of Nuit, this formula adds blood as its fifth ingredient. This is also the recipe for the sacramental 'cakes of light'.

Chapter III of *The Book of the Law* is the most challenging, especially if you interpret it literally. I firmly believe that approach to be an error: it speaks primarily on archetypal, allegorical levels of an inner war that we each must wage within our own lives and characters. Ra-Hoor-Khuit personifies a social and spiritual impetus that demands real change and fundamental transformation, both individually and as a species.

As the 'visible **object** of worship', he is a tangible spiritual **objective**: a common spiritual goal that all people seek under widely varied names, attributes, and methods of worship, the spiritual sun (or star) at the heart of the human soul, the interior initiator and hierophant, the one solar force expressing itself with infinite diversity.

'Every man and every woman is a star.' We previously learned that Hadit is 'the flame that burns in every heart of man, and in the core of every star' and that Nuit is 'Infinite Space, and the Infinite Stars thereof'. Ra-Hoor-Khuit, as child and star, mirrors the idea that **we, who are stars, are ourselves children of Nuit and Hadit**, abiding in relationship to both the infinite without and the infinite within. At our individual centres shines Hadit, and, collectively, we are the 'infinite stars' comprised by Nuit.

Significantly, therefore, Ra-Hoor-Khuit symbolizes this **union of complements**. Chapter III begins with the word Abrahadabra, a Qabalistic code meaning **completion and fulfilment** that arises from the intimate union of opposites, especially the opposites of microcosm and macrocosm. Therefore, he is much the same symbol as the rosy cross, which portrays flowering immortal, enduring love **joined at**

a common centre with a symbol of mortal life extended outward, in all directions, into the world; that is, **a union of love and will**.

AND THE REST OF THE GANG

BABALON & THERION

BABALON

I would give my odds that you had already heard this name before at 50/50. Maybe even more than that. Truth is, Babalon is one of the most recognizable names in occulture nowadays, and I argue it's been the case since the publication of Peter Grey's seminal *The Red Goddess* in 2007. A flawed book, and one that has been taken as gospel by many without much further analysis, it only speaks of Grey's own interpretation of an incredibly complex egregore.[24] Let's see if we can unpack it a little together.

To do so, we must look at Crowley's personal history. He was born in a family belonging to the Exclusive Brethren, an even more radical sect within the Plymouth Brethren – and they were (and still are) a rather radical Christian sect that maintained the belief that the Bible is the supreme authority for church doctrine and practice, over and above any other source of authority. Plymouth Brethren generally see themselves as a network of like-minded free churches, not as a Christian denomination.

The Bible was his sole reading material for all his infancy and adolescence. Exhibiting a rebellious streak from a very young age, his mother dubbed him 'The Beast', which not only gave way to another egregore we will meet later on but also made sure that the *Book of Revelation* of St John became Aleister's favourite one.

It's in the apocalyptic visions of the mystic of Patmos that we find the first mention of Babalon, here depicted as the Whore of Babylon:

> … and I saw a woman sit upon a scarlet coloured beast, full of names of blasphemy, having seven heads and ten horns.
>
> And the woman was arrayed in purple and scarlet colour, and decked with gold and precious stones and pearls, having a golden cup in her hand full of abominations and filthiness of her fornication:

---

[24] An egregore is an esoteric idea that represents a non-physical entity that emerges from the collective thoughts of a certain group of individuals. Historically, the term refers to heavenly entities, or watchers, and the rites and activities connected with them, namely within Enochian traditions.

More recently, the notion has referred to a psychic manifestation, or thoughtform, that occurs when any group has a shared motivation – being composed of, and affecting, the group's thoughts.

And upon her forehead was a name written, MYSTERY,
BABYLON THE GREAT, THE MOTHER OF HARLOTS
AND ABOMINATIONS OF THE EARTH.

And I saw the woman drunken with the blood of the saints,
and with the blood of the martyrs of Jesus: and when I saw her,
I wondered with great admiration.[25]

The end of something is always the beginning of something new.
According to the theory of aeonics we discussed earlier, the end
of the Christian era represented the beginning of the Thelemic
aeon. And those demonized in Christian scripture became the
heroes and gods of this new era. The Whore of Babylon was set
to become the Earthly counterpart of Nuit herself – Babalon is
indeed Nuit's 'secret name' mentioned in *Liber AL* I.22.

However, before that she appeared somewhere else first.

During a tour to Southern Bohemia (now Czech Republic)
in 1587, the great scholar and magician John Dee and
his associate Edward Kelly performed a series of magical
workings, including Kelly scrying for visions in a black
obsidian mirror. Finally, they established contact with an
entity known as Madimi, who appeared as a little girl and
gave Kelly a vision:

I am the daughter of Fortitude, and ravished every hour from my
youth. For behold I am Understanding and science dwelleth in me;
and the heavens oppress me.

They cover and desire me with infinite appetite; for none
that are earthly have embraced me, for I am shadowed with the
Circle of the Stars and covered with the morning clouds ...[26]

---

[25] *Revelation* 17:3–4

[26] Meric Casaubon (editor), *A True & Faithful Relation of what passed for many Yeers
Between Dr John Dee ... and Some Spirits* (London, 1659).

It will be in the angelic conversations of Dee and Kelly, the basis of the Enochian system of magic, that the name Babalon first appears as the Enochian word *babalond*, meaning 'wicked, harlot'. The vision granted to Kelly is similar to that of the unnamed goddess of the ancient Coptic text *The Thunder, Perfect Mind*, one of the manuscripts found at the Nag Hammadi library in 1945.

Following his own experimentations with the Enochian system alongside his lover and disciple **Victor Neuburg**,[27] Crowley began to focus more and more on Babalon as a predominant figure in the still-developing Thelemic theology. Being identified with Binah on the Tree of Life and thus residing above the Qabalistic abyss, she is the new redeemer that beckons the aspirants to initiation to embrace the law of Thelema and reach her in complete understanding. She is akin to Shakti, the secret power underlying all of creation and found, sleeping, within our very selves. She is the holder of the Holy Graal, so the initiate is called to set out on a mythical quest to find her, as did the knights of the Arthurian myth. She is considered a sacred whore because she denies no one, yet she extracts a great price – the blood of the adepts and their ego-identity as earthly individuals. This aspect of Babalon is described further from the vision of the 12th Enochian aethyr in Crowley's *The Vision and the Voice*.

It's there that we learn that the mystery of Babalon – described as the mother of abominations, in true iconoclastic fashion – is that of 'adulteries', since she is the one wilfully making herself a slave to every experience possible, becoming the mistress of all that there is to be experienced. It's also here that we learn another name for her: Understanding. This is a

---

[27] Victor Benjamin Neuburg (6 May 1883–31 May 1940) was an English poet and writer. He also wrote on the subjects of theosophy and occultism. Aside from his connection with Crowley, he's remembered as the publisher of the early works of Pamela Hansford Johnson and Dylan Thomas. (*Wikipedia*)

translation of the term Binah – the third sephirah on the Tree of Life and the first of the supernal.

The mysteries of Babalon are, indeed, the true gateway into humanity's final initiation.

One could write an entire book on Babalon alone, and many have tried, to different degrees of success, starting with the one mentioned at the beginning of this chapter. You will find a selection in the reading suggestions at the end of this book, but one that merits mention here is *Liber 49*, a channelled text that its author considered to be the fourth lost chapter of *Liber AL vel Legis*.

The author was **Jack Parsons,** one of the principal founders of the Jet Propulsion Laboratory and the Aerojet Engineering Corporation. Besides being responsible for creating the fuel that would eventually bring mankind to the moon and back, Parsons was also a dedicated Thelemite. He and Crowley never met but exchanged correspondence during the time Parsons led the Los Angeles branch of the Ordo Templi Orientis,[28] one of the organizations that Crowley was in charge of. Veering between considering him a genius and a fool, in the end Crowley would

---

[28] Ordo Templi Orientis (OTO, literally 'Order of the Temple of the East') is an occult initiatory organization founded at the beginning of the 20th century. The origins of the OTO can be traced back to the German-speaking occultists Carl Kellner, Heinrich Klein, Franz Hartmann and Theodor Reuss. Later, the OTO was significantly shaped by the English author and occultist Aleister Crowley.

After Crowley's death in 1947, four main branches of the OTO have claimed exclusive descent from the original organization and primacy over the other ones. The most visible of these is the Caliphate OTO, incorporated by Crowley's student Grady McMurtry in 1979.

Originally it was intended to be modelled after and associated with European Freemasonry, such as Masonic Templar organizations, and the Egyptian Rites but under the leadership of Aleister Crowley, OTO was reorganized around Thelema as its central metaphysical principle. One of the major features and core teachings of the organization is its practice of sex magick. (*Wikipedia*)

disown him after Parsons embarked on a complex magical operation aimed at bringing a god down to our plane of existence.

Parsons would carry on, and he would consider the operation successful when a beautiful young woman with fiery hair appeared on his doorstep: she was Marjorie Cameron, who would go on to become a famous actress and artist in her own right. If you think this is outlandish, you will be even more surprised to learn that Parsons' magical partner and aide in this operation was a certain **Lafayette Ron Hubbard**. The same individual would take all he learned in his brief time as a Thelemite, as a member of Parson's Agape Lodge, modify it heavily, and create one of the most enduring, wealthy, and noxious cults of contemporary history: Scientology.

In conclusion: Babalon is a multifaceted and incredibly complex egregore that defies every attempt to pigeonhole her. She is not a 'goddess' *per se*, but pure understanding. She will undeniably come to you in her own ways. Always be aware of this, and don't fall into the trap of thinking your own gnosis is everyone else's: this is the fundamental problem of casting Babalon solely as a feminist icon. It's undeniable that she also embodies that role, but to think that's all she is is disingenuous at best.

She is a vector of transcendence. By virtue of that, she accepts *all* in her cup. Through her, if we can heed her call across the abyss and beyond the ordeals found therein, we leave magick behind for good and fully embrace the other side of the coin: mysticism. But this is a story for another time and another book.

THERION

You can breathe now ... there isn't nearly as much to say about the rest of the gang. Thelema is barely over 100 years old, and we are still trying to make sense of it. It would be wrong, however, not to give a little spotlight to these other figures that you will meet during your journeys under will.

Therion is a Greek term that means 'beast', and the reference is apparent. We are once again in apocalyptic territories, and we are talking about the Beast of *Revelation*. Qabalistically, Therion is Chokmah to Babalon's Binah, and another of his names is Chaos since it breaks the perfect unity of Kether. And we can infer that if Babalon is Shakti, then Therion is equivalent to Shiva, understood as the divine will, which manifests all that there is in mystical marriage with his consort.

Crowley took the name **To Mega Therion** (Greek: 'The Great Beast', which numerates 666) once he reached one of the highest levels of spiritual initiation.

Above: Aiwass, as interpreted by AI algorithms.

AIWASS

Aiwass first appeared during the three days of the writing of *Liber AL vel Legis*, where he identifies himself as 'the minister of Hoor-Paar-Kraat' – the passive form of Horus. Once again, I urge you to fight the temptation of placing these larger-than-life characters into neat little boxes. Instead, consider that spirits and gods, who aren't bound to human bodies and the shackles of space and time, can exist as different aspects simultaneously.

Crowley himself struggled his entire life with whether Aiwass was a part of himself or a completely external, independent being. He was sure this being possessed knowledge vaster than he could ever hope for and eventually identified Aiwass with his own Holy Guardian Angel. More on the nature of the Holy Guardian Angel later.

In *Magick in Theory and Practice*, Aiwass is firmly identified by Crowley as 'The Devil', 'Satan', and 'Lucifer', whose 'emblem is Baphomet':

> This serpent, SATAN, is not humanity's adversary, but He who created the Gods of our myths, understanding Good and Evil; He commanded 'Know Thyself!' and taught initiation. His symbol is BAPHOMET, the Androgyne who is the hieroglyph of arcane perfection.

BAPHOMET

Historically, his first appearance is with the Knights Templar; he was described by the Inquisition as the pagan idol the disgraced knights worshipped while in Jerusalem.

Fast-forward to 1856, the French occultist Éliphas Lévi drew his famous picture of the sabbatic goat, representing the 'symbolization of the equilibrium of opposites'. His intention was to describe the goal of perfect social order. A few decades later, Baphomet would enter the Thelemic canon first in *Liber XV: The Gnostic Mass*, written by Crowley, where in its creed we read: 'And I believe in the Serpent and the Lion, Mystery of Mysteries, in His name BAPHOMET.'

The lion is Meithras, and the serpent is Abraxas. Together, they become Chnoubis, yet another name for Baphomet. The

BAPHOMET

lion-serpent symbol complex is very ancient and occurs in Mithraic, Egyptian, and Gnostic iconography.

While many over the years have insisted that Baphomet is an evil deity, in Thelema we see him as the union of opposites: the union of Chaos and Babalon. Philosophically, it represents the synthesis of thesis and antithesis. Qabalistically, Chokhmah and Binah united in Tiphareth.

PAN

Pan is the Greek god of nature, passion, and masculine creative force. He is playful and lecherous. Pan's presence in Thelema, like Babalon and Baphomet's, identifies the sexual undercurrents of the new aeon's magical formulae.

PAN

Pan is a Greek word that also means 'all'. As a result, he is a universal symbol, a personification of both nature and cosmos. He is also known as Pangenetor, which means 'all-begetter', and Panphage, which means 'all-devourer'. As a result, Pan is both the giver and taker of life. In a broader sense, it is the state in which one overcomes all constraints and feels one with the universe.

In *The Book of Lies*, a series of mystical instructions for very advanced initiates, Pan appears several times. There is a hint of the **Night of Pan**, a metaphysical stage that will play a critical role in the most advanced Thelemic initiation. In the same text, there are also references to the 'Comedy of Pan', that is, life itself with its seemingly irreconcilable differences. Only those who have found their True Will, recognized the duality of the embodied experience, can hope to transcend it and become a joyous actor on the sempiternal stage of existence itself.

TRUE WILL, THE HOLY GUARDIAN ANGEL, AND THE ABYSS

Now that we have established Thelema in time and introduced some of its most important characters, we must focus squarely on its absolute protagonist: you.

I hope I have been successful in laying the hints all around the text so far, but if I failed, this is where I say the quiet part out loud. In this new aeon, you are the central character of the epic. Not gods or heroes: you, and you alone. This is the groundbreaking change of perspective that brings each individual to the centre of the universe, as each becomes essentially one with the interplay between Hadit and Nuit, as we saw earlier. There is no saviour to pray to, no vicarious atonement. In fact, there is nothing to be saved from either – only fantastic adventures to be had, both on this plane of existence and on others.

Magick is the tool to use to fully embrace this new perspective. The practices of the previous chapters, which led you to build your magical pyramid, will help you strengthen the bond with your Holy Guardian Angel, who has always been there, waiting for you to attune your senses to their constant calls. If you have diligently worked through those exercises and given yourself enough time to dive into them without being drowned in overthinking the whys and hows of it all, in time you will be ready to attempt the more complex rituals devised to formalize such union. I will briefly discuss Crowley's blueprint for this operation, called **Liber Samekh**. I won't, however, go too much into detail, as the Knowledge and Conversation of the Holy Guardian Angel (shortened to K&CHGA) goes beyond the scope of a book squarely aimed at beginners. I believe it's important to underline that many mistake the K&CHGA with a much earlier stage called the 'vision of the angel'. When you start getting serious about magick and initiation – that is, when you get to this point in a book like this, more or less – you can expect to start getting glimpses, visions, and dreams about the angel calling you incessantly. You may even get a name, a sigil, or something that makes you believe you have united with the HGA. I urge you not to fall into the trap of thinking you can avoid the Great Work altogether, or even worse, falling into the delusion of the *chosen one syndrome*.

Discovering your True Will and achieving the union with the angel is not where Thelema ends. Instead, I argue it's where it actually begins. Qabalistically, the new aeon pushes the end of the initiatory journey upwards on the Tree of Life: not in Tiphereth any more, but in Binah – beyond the dreaded abyss. These new pathways to explore, and the chance to achieve even higher states of consciousness, are the defining characteristics of that better and faster operating system the universe installed at the dawn of the aeon of Horus.

This is the work of the **adept** – so don't worry about it for now. I will only describe it a little for the sake of completion.

Imagine it: you've built your magical pyramid, unlocked the quintessence, united with your Holy Guardian Angel, and now reside in Heliopolis, the City of the Sun. From there, you know that death is but an illusion, and you are finally in perfect balance, the lower reflected in the higher and vice versa. *Solve et Coagula*, as Baphomet reminds us.

This is when you are called to embark on a new, final quest. To do so, you must unbalance yourself willingly. From the perfect beauty of Tiphereth, you are called to experience both the martial fury of Geburah and then the prosperous stability of Chesed. And then, you are faced with the most difficult choice: to let go of all you have experienced so far, even the angel itself, and fling yourself into the abyss, an infinite desert between you and your destination.

The dweller in the abyss is **Choronzon**, but to call it an individual would be wrong. The abyss is empty of being and yet filled with all possible forms, each evil in the only true sense of the word – meaningless but malignant, in so far as it craves to become real. Choronzon is not a demon, adversary, or anything you can truly fight. It is **dispersion**: the loss of focus, the lack of motivation, the countless hours spent on social media replying to every nasty comment on YouTube or Twitter. Choronzon will force you to interrogate yourself in an internal monologue without end. Choronzon is incapable of imagining anything outside itself.

Only through detachment and surrender, by relinquishing the last drop of your blood in the cup of Babalon, will you win this ordeal and finally reach your destination: the City of the Pyramids, under the Night of Pan.

WHY I CAN'T SHOW YOU THE RITUALS OF ALEISTER CROWLEY (AND WHERE YOU CAN FIND THEM)

It's time to address the elephant in the room. Throughout the book, and especially in this chapter, I always tried to paraphrase Crowley's words to minimize quoting directly from him. A big part of this editorial decision was to show that one can indeed distil the essence of Thelema without constantly referring to its founder. If this magical philosophy wants to have a chance to stand the test of time, it must learn to stand on its own legs.

Getting to this point without direct access to Crowley's written material has been challenging but doable so far. We are now going to see if it will be possible for me to try and explain to you the final *Libri* ahead without printing their exact wording.

The good news is that this material is freely available on the internet. I will provide you with a string to input into Google for each of them so you can be sure to get the correct one.

LIBER AL VEL LEGIS & THE HOLY BOOKS OF THELEMA

🌐 Google: *Aleister Crowley Liber AL hermetic.com.*

If you were to strip out of Thelema everything else keeping only one thing, that should be *Liber AL vel Legis* (shortened to *AL*). We have encountered this text throughout the book, and it's time to take a closer look. By now, it should be clear that the reception of this Holy Book kick-started the aeon of Horus. However, Crowley fought against recognizing it as such for many years, to the point that contemporary critics insisted that he made it all up. And while there are indeed some incongruences with the story he told over the years and that most Thelemites are familiar with, from my perspective, it remains one we, as magicians, can work with on a mythical level – especially since the book is full of practical magical and mystical teachings if you know where to look for them, as we noticed while introducing Nuit, Hadit, and Ra-Hoor-Khuit.

One enduring myth about *AL* is that you must never discuss its contents and destroy your copy after reading it. These ideas come directly from the so-called 'new comment': a few paragraphs you will find at the end of most, if not all, versions of *AL* you can purchase in a bookstore. This was Crowley's last attempt to fulfil the exhortation found in the book that charged him to write a comment for all to fully understand its meaning. He tried for many years, sometimes successfully, sometimes interpreting the messages of *AL* in a very unsavoury manner, and, in the end, he would consider all these attempts as 'some of the most turgid hogwash' he ever penned. That's when this final new comment came into being. On a surface level, it basically tells us that *AL* is dangerous, and we should never discuss it lest we become 'centres of pestilence'.

So dangerous, in fact, that the only reasonable thing to do once we've read the text is to destroy it. You can find plenty of stories floating around online of Thelemites, both famous and unknown, who did precisely that.

To me, those who follow the instruction of the new comment to the letter completely fail the intelligence test it hides. To believe that Thelemites are forbidden to fully engage and discuss with their main text is ridiculous at best and worrying to a degree when you realize how this intimation has been used by various Thelemic organizations to stifle growth and silence dissenters.

To those with eyes to see, it will become evident that a comment that starts with 'Do what thou wilt shall be the whole of the Law' and ends with 'There is no law beyond Do what thou wilt' while forcing upon you specific and restrictive limitations in the intervening paragraphs, is indeed nothing more than a test. And now you know how to cheat it.

AL is not the sole sacred text of Thelema, however. Initially published in 1909 by Crowley under the title *Θελημα*, they make up the Class A of official instructions, which indicates that they are not to be changed, even to the letter. Instead, they are to be considered as inspired or channelled works, not so much written by Crowley but through him.

Here's the complete list – they can all be found online:

- *Liber AL vel Legis* commonly called *The Book of the Law*.
- *Liber LXV Cordis Cincti Serpente sub figurâ* אדני . Details the aspirant's relationship with their Holy Guardian Angel.
- *Liber Liberi vel Lapidis Lazuli, Adumbratio Kabbalae Aegyptiorum sub figurâ VII.* The first steps of a Master of the Temple. Its seven chapters are referred to the seven heavenly bodies in the following order: Mars, Saturn, Jupiter, Sol, Mercury, Luna, and Venus.
- *Liber Trigrammaton sub figurâ XXVII.* It describes the trigrams of the mutations of the *tao* through yin and yang, and the cosmic process as a whole.

- *Liber DCCCXIII vel Ararita sub figurâ DLXX.* An explanation of the hexagram and how to reduce it to unity and beyond. This book covers a very secret initiation procedure in magical terminology.
- *Liber B vel Magi sub figurâ I.* A description of the grade of Magus, the highest grade that may be manifested in any fashion in this realm.
- *Liber Porta Lucis sub figurâ X.* A narrative of the A∴A∴ dispatching of Master Therion and an explanation of his task.
- *Liber Stellæ Rubeæ sub figurâ LXVI.* Symbolic sexual magick.
- *Liber Tzaddi (צ) vel Hamus Hermeticus sub figurâ XC.* A narrative of initiation and an indication of those who are qualified for it.
- *Liber Cheth (ח) vel Vallum Abiegni sub figurâ CLVI.* Symbolic sexual magick.
- *Liber Arcanorum τών Atu τού Tahuti Quas Vidit Asar In Amennti sub figurâ CCXXXI Liber Carcerorum τών Qliphoth cum suis Geniis.* A description of the cosmic process as depicted by the tarot trumps. The sequence of the 22 trumps is stated as an initiating formula.
- *Liber A'ash (עש) vel Capricorni Pneumatici sub figurâ CCCLXX.* Analyzes the nature of mankind's creative magical energy, explains how to awaken and employ it, and identifies the general and specific things received as a result. Sexual magick hidden under symbology.
- *Liber Tau (ת) vel Kabbalæ Trium Literarum.* A pictorial interpretation of the initiated tarot.

As you can easily see, these are an incredibly diverse selection of themes. The one I would select for a beginner is *Liber Tzaddi.* Also called *the Hermetic Fish-Hook* (*tzaddi* means 'fish-hook' in Hebrew), it gives one of the most enlightening and inspiring introductions to the concept of initiation. And it charges you to recognize that your constant companion on this lifelong path is yourself (which also implies the angel), as well as insisting that proper initiation can only be reached by marrying the highest with the lowest, the light with the darkness, the beautiful with the ugly. It's the alchemical concordance of the opposites that creates something bigger than the sum of its parts. Last but not least, it teaches you to seek what you usually are not attracted to: only by engaging with what we seem to dislike can we achieve full enlightenment.

LIBER V VEL REGULI: THE RITUAL OF THE MARK OF THE BEAST

Google: *Aleister Crowley Liber V vel Reguli hermetic.com.*
With *Liber V vel Reguli* (abbreviated to *Reguli*), it's finally time to start looking at the Thelemic counterparts and evolutions of the pentagram and the hexagram.

The first problem we encounter is that in stark difference from the rituals we have studied and practised so far, many comments and precise instructions about them in Crowley's extensive opus don't seem to exist. At least, not publicly.

So you can easily imagine how a quick Google search will bring you dozens of different interpretations without any chance to correctly determine which one is valid and which isn't. My suggestion, as usual, is to learn by doing – while constantly studying the lessons of the Thelemic Holy Books. Crowley left countless hints across all of his writings, and while searching for them might seem daunting, it will also be gratifying.

With this bit of preamble out of the way, let me share with you my own interpretations, borne from over two decades of experiments and the excellent tutorship of my teachers.

Reguli is an 'incantation proper to invoke the energies of the aeon of Horus, adapted for the daily use of the magician of whatever grade'. Crowley also uses a strange term, *animadversion*, to describe it. In English, its meaning is that of criticism or censure. However, it comes ultimately from the Latin phrase *animum advertere*, meaning 'to turn the mind to'.

In this light, it becomes clear that this should be your first Thelemic ritual if we discount the daily solar adorations. It's appropriate for everyone, from the newbie neophyte to the advanced adept, and it's engineered to rewire your body of light to function with the energies of the new aeon – the *93 current* (yes, you can think of it precisely as a kind of electric current!)

There are different elemental attributions to the four quarters: Air is now to the north, Earth to the east, while Fire and Water remain unchanged. You are moving *widdershins* instead of *deosil*.[29] Also, the pentagrams you are tracing are *averse*, which alongside the ritual's 'subtitle' in reference to the *Mark of the Beast*, gives it a sulphurous vibe.

By now, I hope I have convinced you that the Luciferian tints of Thelema are there to underline a radical rethinking of our approach to initiation and spirituality. These changes are meant to signify that, in the new aeon, the spirit is finally able to fully descend into matter, and the two are indeed one and the same. And the difference in position of the four cardinal signs of the zodiac in *Reguli* is Crowley's way of reaffirming the heliocentric nature of Thelema and thus its adherents. I must thank Lon Milo DuQuette and his now-classic *The Magick of Aleister Crowley* for stating out loud that *Reguli* doesn't turn the belt of the zodiac, or the pentagrams, upside down … but the magician. And it imparts the lesson that our true essence exists out there, rather than being chained to Earth.

This ritual also introduces its own reduced version of a middle pillar practice, the signs of NOX, which will be explored further in the *Star Ruby*, and several Thelemic formulae, the most important of which is *LAShTAL*. Crowley's commentary

---

29 Widdershins is a term meaning to go counter-clockwise, to go anti-clockwise, or to go lefthandwise, or to walk around an object by always keeping it on the left. Literally, it means to take a course opposite the apparent motion of the sun viewed from the northern hemisphere (the centre of this imaginary clock is the ground the viewer stands upon). The opposite of widdershins is deosil, or sunwise, meaning 'clockwise'. (*Wikipedia*)

LIBER V VEL REGULI

THE MARK OF THE BEAST

Above: The stations and the dance of *Liber V vel Reguli*

goes into much depth about it, and I definitely suggest you take some time to study it. It's one of the most profound pieces of Thelemic thought and expands on the necessity for the magician to constantly analyze the universe in terms of polarities to bring them to annihilation and move away from the deceptions of a dualistic viewpoint.

THE STAR RUBY & THE FORMULA OF NOX

 Google: *Aleister Crowley Liber XXV: the Star Ruby hermetic.com.*

The *Star Ruby* is the first of the two rituals (the other being the *Star Sapphire*) where Crowley only comments something along the lines that it would be improper to comment on it at all.

LIBER XXV

THE STAR RUBY

Above: The stations and the energies of the *Star Ruby*

Thanks for nothing, Uncle Al!

This approach led many to believe that only by joining either the A∴A∴ or the OTO could one genuinely learn how to unlock the secrets of these rituals. Others inferred that, because of Crowley's insistence on avoiding explanations, he littered these rituals with double blinds to confuse the uninitiated. The reality is that very few notes and diary entries survive at all.

What we know for sure is that he considered the *Star Ruby* as the rewritten and more elaborate version of the ritual of the pentagram. First published in 1913 in *The Book of Lies*, a final version appears in 1929 in *Magick in Theory and Practice*, which I will refer to here.

Many find it to be more powerful, more dynamic and likely more dramatic a ritual, to the point of leaving behind the elemental pentagrams and even the greater pentagrams altogether. However, I definitely don't suggest doing so since, in my opinion, the *Star Ruby* operates on a completely different vibrational level than the rituals we've studied so far.

It starts with an exorcism and, to my way of looking, that first movement is the banishing part of the ritual. Furthermore, it requires substantial skill in concentration and visualization as the pentagrams in the four quarters are not physically traced before oneself but instead envisioned fully formed. Finally, the archangels are replaced by Neoplatonic divine principles based on the *Chaldean Oracles*, a text that should be studied by those undertaking the performance of this ritual.

So … where does the *Star Ruby* operate then? First, attention should be paid to the particular instructions for the name's delivery. They are not merely vibrated. Instead, the magician is instructed to **roar THERION** in the east, **say NUIT** in the north, **whisper BABALON** in the west, and finally **bellow HADIT** in the south. This characterizes the feel of these egregores but also possibly hints at something else.

IUNGES

DAIMONES

SYNOCHES

TELETARCHAI

Above: Suggestion for visualizing the divine principles
of the *Chaldean Oracles*

Maybe we can make sense of this puzzle a bit more if we look at the four cherubim and make up the image of the hermetic sphinx.

It's a lion who roars; traditionally, the lion is attributed to the element Fire. Man can be attributed to the element Air. Whispers suggest sensuality, and thus the element Water. Finally, a bull bellows, thus indicating the element Earth. And here, we have a different set of correspondences: Fire for east, Air for north, Water for west, and Earth for south. These are the sidereal attributions, but with Water and Air reversed. Is this a similar situation to the one we encountered just above, discussing *Reguli*?

Another school of thought insists that the magician shouldn't think of the classical elements while performing the *Star Ruby*. After all, you are not invoking or banishing the elements but invoking the Thelemic egregores. So while moving into quarters, the element stays the same, but it's the magician that brings another element to create an alchemical mixture of the two, to fuel the invocation. So you will have the Fire of Air to invoke Therion, the Air of Earth to invoke Nuit, the Water of Water to invoke Babalon, and finally, the Earth of Fire to invoke Hadit. The tarot aficionado will have undoubtedly already seen something: those are court cards, respectively the Knight of Swords, Prince of Disks, Queen of Cups and Princess of Wands.

As you are trying to solve the puzzle of the quarters, you are faced with a bigger mystery: **the formula of NOX**. The signs of NOX are attributed to the A∴A∴ adept grades. Each represents one step from Tiphereth to Binah, from the grade of Adeptus Minor to that of Magister Templi. Alongside the intimation to use them while chanting a **paean** – a song of praise to Pan – the fundamental goal of this powerful ritual suddenly becomes crystal clear: it's an engine for the final initiation and for reaching the City of the Pyramids.

NOX SIGN

PUER

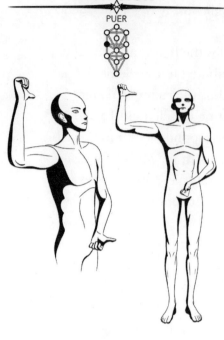

NOX SIGN

VIR

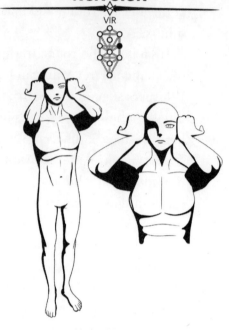

NOX SIGN

PUELLA

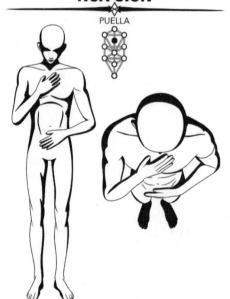

NOX SIGN

MULIER

NOX SIGN

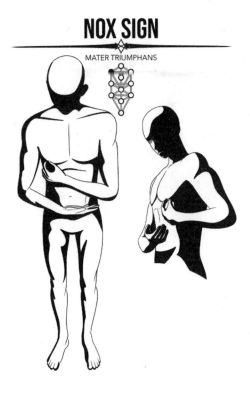

MATER TRIUMPHANS

Above and opposite: the signs of NOX

It's also finally evident why Crowley considered it a better and more powerful version of the pentagram – while the pentagram refined the elements of the magician for them to build their own pyramid, the *Star Ruby* implies the very construction of that pyramid already, the mastery of the powers of the sphinx, and the readiness to embark on the journey across the abyss.

Above: A possible interpretation of the formula
hidden in the *Star Ruby*

THE STAR SAPPHIRE: SEX MAGICK

🌐 Google: *Aleister Crowley Liber XXXVI: the Star Sapphire hermetic.com*.

Just as chapter 25 (5 x 5 = 25) of *The Book of Lies* presented
the *Star Ruby* as a revised pentagram ritual, chapter 36
(6 x 6 = 36) of the same book gave the *Star Sapphire* as a
revised hexagram ritual.

Crowley describes it as 'the real and perfect ritual of the
hexagram', but it doesn't give us any further help. The instructions
in the text are cryptic on crucial points (such as the exact nature of
the 'Holy Hexagram' and the signs to be shown during the ritual).
Indeed, this is another magical puzzle requiring study across
various texts and perhaps even initiated insight.

It begins with: 'Let the adept be armed with his Magick
Rood (and provided with his Mystic Rose).' And thus, those
performing this ritual are exclusively those who have achieved

LIBER XXXVI

THE STAR SAPPHIRE

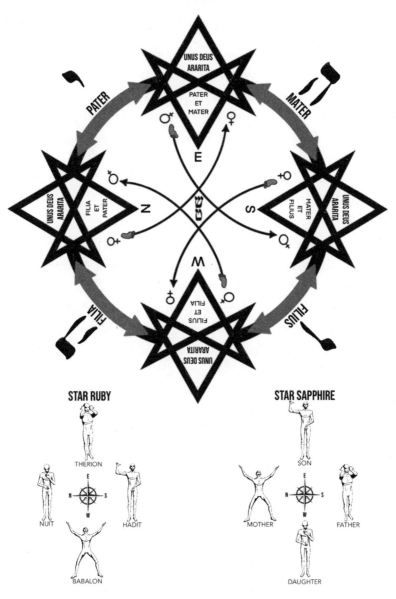

Above: The stations and movements of the *Star Sapphire*, and the differences in orientations of the signs of NOX between the *Star Ruby* and the *Star Sapphire*

the union with the angel. Furthermore, the references to the magick rood and the mystic rose leave no doubts regarding the *Star Sapphire* being an instruction on sex magick. Finally, while several Thelemites still insist that one can perform this ritual also ceremonially and alone, I am ready to bet that every time someone argues this way, Crowley turns in his grave (well, if he had one – he was cremated, and his ashes scattered).

Discussing the details of this ritual goes far beyond this book's scope.[30] I know, what a let-down! I will leave you with some potentially enlightening images. Each one represents one of the four stations of the ritual.

LIBER SAMEKH: A BLUEPRINT, NOT A RECIPE

🌐 Google: *Aleister Crowley Liber Samekh hermetic.com.*
Crowley clearly states many times, across several books and in his diaries, that the most critical magical operation to undertake is the ritual that creates and solidifies the union with the Holy Guardian Angel. He insists – and I agree with him – that until this is achieved, no magick can genuinely be considered efficacious or trustworthy. Yes, your sigil may hit the mark once or twice. Your prayers may be answered. But only after knowing the angel do you enter a perfect harmony with the rest of the universe that allows your True Will, now fully known, to be done.

---

[30] Should you want to look deeper into this subject, try and find a copy of *Ararita: Elaborations On The Star Sapphire*, by someone calling themselves 'A Traveller In Darkness'.

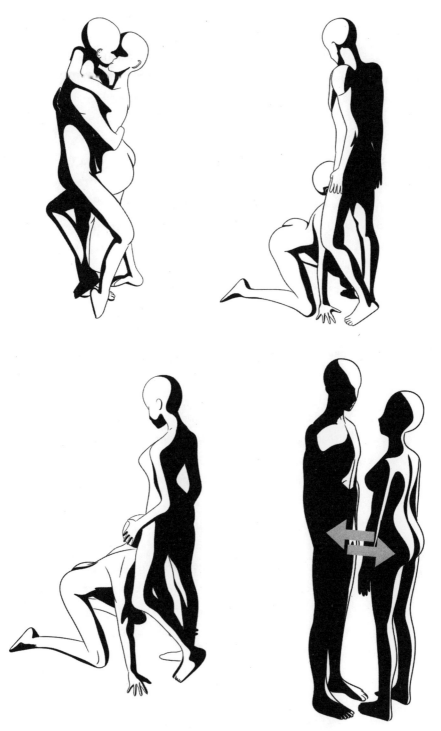

Above: The four stations of the Star Sapphire

IS THE HGA INTERNAL OR EXTERNAL?

At the beginning of this book, I briefly introduced the concept of the Holy Guardian Angel. There we saw how this idea is way older than Crowley or Thelema, and a version of it can be found in most cultures and religions.

I told you how Crowley ping-ponged between considering the HGA internal (for most of his life) and eventually external to himself. Finally, in chapter 43 of *Magick Without Tears*, he says that the HGA is emphatically not a mere abstraction of yourself – not your 'higher self'.

I personally agree with his position here, and generally, I always tend to agree with an author's later ideas. So to me, it only makes sense: he spent his entire life refining these ideas. Unfortunately, though, it is accurate and undeniable that this position pretty much undermines or flat-out renders invalid a lot of his writing, from the theorems in *Magick in Theory and Practice* to *The Initiated Interpretation of Ceremonial Magic*, an introduction to his edition of *The Lesser Key of Solomon* and probably one of his most cited works (often entirely out of context).

I think it is undoubtedly much easier to understand the HGA as something external. It becomes internal once one unites with it as an act of love. However, when I treated it as something external to myself, it didn't matter whether it was internal or external. It was simply a projection I could study in relation and experience more fully. So perhaps this was Crowley's experience too?[1]

---

[1] I would like to thank Thelemic author Gerald del Campo for many enlightening discussions around this topic.

The Thelemic ritual Crowley devised to facilitate this lofty goal is *Liber Samekh* ... or is it? Inspired by the famous *Book of the Sacred Magic of Abramelin the Mage*, and written in 1921 while at the Abbey of Thelema in Cefalú for one of his disciples, it's one of the most annotated – and yet almost incomprehensible to the uninitiated – magical instructions he ever penned.

Decades after first encountering it, I am still baffled by those who claim to have performed it without anything happening. Possibly because the actual magical instruction is conveyed not so much in the ritual proper, where Crowley tells you which eldritch consonants to shout out (each a Qabalistic puzzle in their own right), but rather in 'Point III', or 'scholion' as he calls it. More than a simple commentary, this is where Crowley drops the goods and tells you that to even attempt *Liber Samekh*, you must have trained extensively, likely for years, in all the practices we have gone through so far. As with the *Star Sapphire*, this ritual is aimed squarely at the adept, not the neophyte. And even then, the ritual *per se* is more like a blueprint than a recipe. After all, it's still impossible to lay down precise rules for this magical operation, as Crowley told us in *One Star In Sight*.

So ... next time you read on social media that someone has attempted *Liber Samekh*, but nothing happened, you can infer they were right out of their depth and maybe too lazy to put in the months and years needed to approach it correctly.

LIBER OZ: THE RIGHTS OF MAN

Google: *Aleister Crowley Liber OZ hermetic.com.*

We can argue that every single Thelemic text has been taken out of context in one way or another. In the case of the Holy Books, we can attribute it to the fact they have been channelled, and likely the spirits who sent down the message couldn't make it any clearer. But, more likely, Crowley's state – constantly inebriated while receiving them – played a more significant role in it.

This cannot be said, however, for *Liber OZ*. Also dubbed 'The Rights of Man' and initially a charge in the ritual of the second degree of the Ordo Templi Orientis, it is one of Crowley's shortest publications. Its primary purpose is to convey the message of the OTO in words of one syllable since Crowley believed that total synthesis was the way to go while trying to share complex ethical, moral, and philosophical ideas with his fellow humans. But, as we saw earlier on with the concept of the Holy Guardian Angel, we can safely say he was dead wrong.

Since the 1980s, alongside the resurgence of outer thelemic organisations, *Liber OZ* has become the go-to banner of Thelemic philosophy – whether you are a member of such organizations, or not. While it's hard to disagree with its tenets, which preach the absolute freedom and liberty of the individual, it also became a shield behind which the ultra-libertarian and the alt-right type of Thelemite hid behind while crying against 'political correctness' or 'cancel culture'.

In more recent years, an in-depth analysis of the text, written by Frater Orpheus, was published. It offered not only the correct historical context, which you cannot divorce the text from (it really was a call to action against Nazism in World War II) but also hinted at possible magical and mystical formulae hidden in plain sight behind its words. While I am not exactly convinced by this theory, especially since the author hides behind the usual veil of initiatory secrecy right before expanding on it, I nevertheless enjoyed considering such a possibility.

Most important to understand is that *Liber OZ* is not, and never was, a 'Class A' text, those considered inviolate and inspired. In fact, Crowley himself never gave it a proper classification at all. And so the fact that most Thelemites out there put more effort into promoting it rather than *Liber AL* itself (or the rest of the Holy Books) gives way to considering that the focus has been likely placed on the wrong one simply because it's the one that doesn't require much thought at all.

There's one final note to make about *Liber OZ*. One of its lines reads: 'There is no god but man.' Many who read it do not realize that, differently from the citations from *Liber AL* coming right before it, this one is not a quote from any of the Holy Books. So, again, it's not doctrine. But, interestingly, this line has given way for some to insist that Thelema is by default atheistic. One of the most monolithic supporters of this idea is my good friend, the Thelemic author (and rock star) Rodney Orpheus (who *is not* the same Frater Orpheus as above). Once again, I am not convinced at all: the way I read it is that in the new aeon, the individual is the only god left. Your mileage may vary.

TETELESTAI!

CHAPTER 7

TETELESTAI!

That's Greek, and it means: 'It is done!'

Now that it is done, let me share another secret with you: I never thought I would be able to finish this book, this writing endeavour. And yet here we are, at the finish line.

I hope you enjoyed the run as much as I did while preparing and sharing it with you. The practices you have learned will serve you throughout your life, and you should be confident that, if you stick to the plan, you'll be able to start to explore what else is out there and discover exactly how deep the rabbit hole goes.

Before we say our goodbyes, let me answer some of the questions you might have at this point. But, wait, how do I know you have these questions? Magick, of course!

SHOULD I JOIN A MAGICAL ORDER?

Someone once remarked that 'a magician without a magical order was like a politician without a political party.' I have long thought that was an apt observation, and I found that it explained, and even justified, why most of us tolerated the tedium and trials of participation in magical groups.

In recent years, and after some awful experiences, I have come to revise my opinion. Éliphas Lévi wrote some of the most influential texts on occultism we have, as you have surely noticed by now, given how much I quoted from his writings. Crowley considered him to be one of his previous incarnations. Still, he was not preoccupied with any magical organization. Indeed, evidence of his membership and participation in occult groups is tenuous at best. What he had to say was never the secret, jealously guarded property of this or that little group. The more we ponder the evidence, it is clear that many great magicians flew solo, and it never compromised either the quality of their work or placed limitations on their clout. If anything, the opposite seems to be true.

I would suggest that participation in these groups can quickly become an enormous distraction for many serious occultists. Rather than focus on their magical work, they try to manage these groups. On the other hand, people without magical talent fiercely nurture the illusion that participating in these often dismal and pedestrian organizations confers some kind of prestige and higher purpose on them and their efforts. All we have to do is open our eyes to see how hollow their pretensions are.

Many will argue that some famous and important occultists did, indeed, devote a great deal of their time and attention to these groups. I suspect that a sceptical investigation will undermine these kinds of assumptions. Crowley preached Ordo Templi Orientis, but did he always practise it? Was he running around trying to organize Gnostic Masses and nursing people through the lower degrees in the 1930s and 1940s? Was he fretting about buying roses for the Gnostic Mass every week in London or Hastings and dealing with all the little minutia those of you who might have had experiences with Ecclesia Gnostica Catholica might be all too familiar with? No, he was not.

If anything, his testy tone to the letters of his followers in California makes me think he resented having to negotiate their petty squabbles – and who can blame him? What would have happened if he had put all that aside and turned to other tasks?

The worse the leaders of these groups are, the more ridiculous the problems these organizations present to anyone with a shred of talent, motivation, and basic integrity. Yes, I am well aware that your local lodge has no issue, and its members are all honest seekers of truth, exactly as you are. However, that is beside the point. Because in strictly hierarchical groups, if the top is rotten, the decay will spread to the rest of the tree – all the time.

If you find yourself, over and over again, fighting with the people in charge of you, if you vacillate between obsequious flattery of the bosses and vicious denunciations of them, then maybe your own psychological condition is the reason you are spinning in this particular hamster wheel.

But, there is a way out. Climb off the wheel. What do you have to lose?

SO I CAN FIND EVERYTHING I NEED ONLINE?

Yes and no.

Indeed, most of the secrets of these magical orders and mystical societies have been published repeatedly since the 1970s. But, of course, the Ordo Templi Orientis is still positioned as the owner of the mystery of mystery, the key to real alchemy and sexual magick. However, **Francis X King**[31] revealed everything Crowley ever wrote on the subject, already 50 years ago in his book *The Secret Rituals of the OTO*.

This is the same for every single one of these 'secrets', without fail.

---

[31] George Francis King (10 January 1934–8 November 1994), known as Francis X King, was a British occult writer and editor from London who wrote about tarot, divination, witchcraft, magic, sex magic, tantra, and holistic medicine. (*Wikipedia*)

One could argue, and rightfully so, that you won't go very far without a mentor that can help you untangle the strange languages and the chimeric allegories of these texts. Even the landmark book by King I just mentioned won't make any sense to you if you don't have a solid masonic AND Thelemic background.

But, at the same time, so many have shared their commentaries in recent years that you only have to put in the hours of study and practice to gain sufficient understanding.

Unfortunately, the other side of the coin is that the amount of disinformation, narcissism, and straight-up grifting you will find online has rapidly become an almost impossible ordeal to win.

We could talk about the dangers of becoming slave to a social media algorithm that wants you to churn out content relentlessly, without care for quality or insight. And how much that puts you under the spotlight in times when the echoes of the Satanic Panic seems suddenly closer than ever.

We could talk about how the need to fill the content hole can result in the same easy tropes of occultism being endlessly repackaged with diminishing returns and without much thought or interrogation into where these ideas came from or why they are there.

We could talk about whether people who are drawn to magick in these sorts of numbers right now actually are being best served by this landscape or if it's just another vector of gig economy exploitation.

We could talk about all this and a lot more, and still, we would only have scratched the surface of all the problems you are likely to find as soon as you log in on Reddit, join a Discord server, or reply to a Twitter thread.

And that's without even touching upon the real and present danger of being exposed to online cults, often hiding beneath a veneer of respectability ('Hey, we are against the evil corporations, and we like permaculture!'). Or the insidious spread of alt-right and far-right ideologies everywhere, but always just one plausible deniability away from picturing those sounding the alarm as witch hunters.

It's hard out there.

THELEMIC HOT TAKES

As I said already, online occulture can be a wild west. Nevertheless, the following questions can give you an idea of the tone you will likely find on Twitter, Reddit, or Facebook groups. And here's my attempt at answering them in good faith.

Don't feel you need to read the Crowley books. They're old, hard to understand, and complicated, plus he uses many words you aren't familiar with. So let it go because that stuff isn't important at all. Instead, read beginner books by people like Lon Milo DuQuette and, if you've been to junior college, Israel Regardie. You'll get all the information there you will ever need.

Obviously, one should read Crowley. All of it. As well as the entirety of the curriculum and syllabus he suggests. Do that, and you will gather a solid basis in occult philosophy. I was lucky to be presented with most of it during my early years, from high school to university. Nowadays, most of those who want to embrace Thelema seem to come from unschooled backgrounds, creating a barrier of entry for many. This book attempts to break some walls – but it's only meant to start your journey! You can continue by checking out the suggestions for further reading at the end of the book. And yes, those include a vast range of authors from Crowley to DuQuette, who remains one of the best promulgators of Thelema ever.

Listen to the people in the community. Don't study books on occultism. Instead, learn from the people around you and take their opinions and ideas seriously. Follow the lead of the people in the group.

I would say do both: reading, studying, and understanding the source material is paramount. So you can also learn how to disagree with it if need be. There is value in listening to the experiences of those who walked the path before you. You should always remain critical of them, however. Thelema should be about leaders, not followers. This brings us to …

Follow the leaders. Protect them from the criticism of others, including your own. Keep quiet and do what you're told.

Absolutely not. While this approach will serve you fine if you want to become a 'careerist magician', rising up in the hierarchies of this or that magical order, coven, or esoteric society, in my experience I also found out it will slow down your own spiritual evolution substantially.

The message of Thelema is that YOU are the protagonist of your own story. Not yet another 'leader' or 'guru' high up on some made-up ladder. I already stated above how Crowley imagined several strict structures for initiation. Still, he himself never really followed any, nor was able to fully flesh them out in a way that's adherent to the new aeon's tenets.

It's time we move beyond it all entirely.

Make the commitment you feel comfortable with. Don't give money unless you absolutely have to. Thelema is about accepting yourself, so don't feel you need to change at all. Letting others pay for everything is fine.

This one is more multilayered: Thelema is about finding the best version of yourself. That requires a deep-rooted change. However, I don't think that implies overcommitting, especially in financial assets, unless you have extra to spare first.

Magick and Thelema are anything you want them to be. It can be new age, a religion, psychology, 'community theatre', or various combinations. But, on the other hand, if you want to bring in Buddhism, witchcraft, or whatever else you just picked up and dropped, go for it!

Thelema is syncretic by its very nature. Some syncretism will feel out of place if it doesn't satisfy our personal aesthetic … I get it. Crowley himself kept hodging and podging to try and sell his product to anyone who'd listen, and I do argue it never worked for him either. However, I also agree that there are some specific truths in Thelema that will not adhere to reductionist 'love and light new ageism'.

Crowley was racist, sexist, anti-Semitic and misogynist. This means you are free to ignore and disregard anything he said that you don't agree with or that makes you feel uncomfortable.

Crowley was racist, sexist, anti-Semitic and misogynist. He was all these things, and he was awful, especially for his time, too. But also held very 'liberal' and 'progressive' views. He was, in a nutshell, a walking contradiction like most geniuses.

The good news: we can move beyond Crowley. In the sense that Thelema wants us to find and do OUR Will, not Crowley's. And he can and should be criticized wildly and eventually left behind. We don't need a new Sky Daddy, and if we do … time to re-examine our priorities.

Thelema is about equality. That means no one is better than you, and no one can criticize you about anything.

Thelema is about finding and then enacting the best version of yourself. But that's a goal, not a starting point. So, of course, you will be prone to criticism, again and again. Take it in, learn from it. And if the person who criticizes you isn't able to do it constructively, block them into oblivion: they will learn a thing or two about remaining in their lanes. Far too many abusive trolls online nowadays.

Your emotions and feelings are what should guide you. If you're angry or upset, listen to that emotion, let it direct you, and justify what you do. It's probably your HGA!

Part of the long and gruesome work needed to find and discover your True Will is to learn to be the master of your emotions and feelings. It is a good idea to keep them under check at all times. This also means directing your anger and rage to the right target so that justice can be served. Remember the lesson of Ra-Hoor-Khuit we discussed above.

Leave any time you want. Thelema isn't about demanding anything from you or asking anything from you.

Yes. Leave any time you want. The lesson of Thelema is to first discover, and then do your True Will. If this leads you to leave behind a group, a fraternity, or even Thelema itself, so be it. What matters is not belonging to a supposedly elite cabal of magicians, but learning how to navigate the experience of life to the fullest.

MAGICK WITHOUT TEARS

At the beginning of this book, I mentioned how the impulse to write it came from the experience of teaching magick during the lockdown years.

The **Magick Without Tears** community still thrives, even now that the world has reopened, and we are trying to ditch that 'new normal' that saw us depending on virtual relationships. If you want, you can find us online – more information on how to join us is located at the end of this chapter.

But which lessons did we collectively learn from this experience?

Many reported that building up a solid parasocial set of relationships through an online group – when everything else failed – was what effectively kept them going. The lockdown years opened doors for those who genuinely want to teach and share their knowledge and those who are honest in their desire to learn in a safe environment. Before, the idea of joining an in-person group was deemed risky by many. Studying these topics in the safety of their own homes (while the world outside hung in a precarious balance) was a welcome change.

Still, because many people had more time, they probably had more opportunities to use social media negatively, such as hexing the moon (yes, this actually happened on TikTok), gaining followers through clickbait or advocating for conspirituality and worse.

Since change and confrontation were part of lockdown times, many recognized how magick helps us deal with those significant events that affect us and that we don't have any direct control over. Furthermore, the practices demonstrated how magick can strengthen and ground us all for similar situations in the future.

Because the pandemic increased access to teachers (via Zoom), several reported that their spiritual growth accelerated because good teachers with whom they would not have been able to take a workshop otherwise (due to geography) were suddenly offering online classes. At the same time, most also reported that it's a pity that so many online options are again disappearing now, which are effectively working toward gatekeeping those who cannot travel due to financial or physical restrictions.

The feedback wasn't always only positive, however.

For some, the feelings about the occult scene haven't changed much – it's flawed, full of problematic individuals, and it's always been like any 'scene'. But on the other hand, their existing perceptions have become more refined and sharpened. If anything, those I talked to now tend to trust people with a podcast, a book deal, or a large social media following less or with more scepticism.

Everyone was clear on one point: they respect and revere magick a lot more now that they know what it's capable of accomplishing for both good and ill, and that it's just plain difficult. However, magick is not to be messed with; it is not a game or a source of entertainment; it transmutes the very stuff that makes us who we think we are, often in unexpected ways. And that's why one must approach it with a solid foundation.

SOLVITUR AMBULANDO

There you go, another strange phrase in a (mainly) dead language. This time it's Latin, meaning 'It is solved by walking'.

Often attributed to St Augustine, one of the most influential philosophers of all time, it's used to pinpoint a problem or a question that can only be resolved by a practical experiment.

And we are now coming full circle from the beginning of our travels together. Once again, the critical point is doing, rather than overthinking, over philosophizing, and overcomplicating your practice to the point of inaction. There are far too many occult book collectors out there. We need more magicians instead.

Through the practices you have learned so far, you can now venture out there with the certainty that you have, at the very least, some solid foundations that will sustain you in your wanderings.

But where to go? If the traditional avenues of finding and joining a magical order aren't ideal any more (and that's an understatement), and if the internet is a constant minefield with few oases of sanity, where can you venture to?

Quite simply, out there in the world.

Magick is something that can be learned in the comfort of your own house. However, once the training is done, you must find the other and learn to interact with it. The only true teacher is the Holy Guardian Angel and its many reverberations across the universe around you.

So step out. You don't have to go 'back to nature' if that's not your thing – it barely is mine. Instead, you can walk the city and learn to speak with its many spirits. Become a mystical *flâneur* and have conversations with the secluded spots no one goes to. Lose yourself in the wandering, and reach out for the 'gentle folk'. Establish faerie embassies. Dare to tread on the corpse roads. That's why you worked to build your body of light. Protection, yes, but also to be recognized as one who seeks the liminal spaces in-between.

Ok, now it's time to really say our goodbyes.

Thank you for your decision to become a magician, and may you be granted the accomplishment of your True Will.

Marco Visconti
24 June 2022 ev
Ad Babalonis Amorem Do Dedico Omnia Nihilo

FURTHER READING

Here's a list of books you might enjoy after this one. They vary from being beginner-friendly to more advanced. Some definitely expect you to be well trained.

THELEMA

Liber AL vel Legis: Centennial Edition by Aleister Crowley
Gems from the Equinox by Israel Regardie
777 by Aleister Crowley
776½: Tables for Practical Ceremonial by James A Eshelman
*Living Thelema: A Practical Guide to Attainment in Aleister Crowley's
    System of Magick* by David Shoemaker
The Magick of Aleister Crowley: A Handbook of the Rituals of Thelema
    by Lon Milo Duquette
The Mystical and Magical System of the A∴A∴ by James A Eshelman
Abrahadabra: Understanding Aleister Crowley's Thelemic Magick by
    Rodney Orpheus
The Heretic's Guide to Thelema by Gerald Del Campo
Liber 49 or The Book of Babalon by Jack Parsons
The Eloquent Blood by Manon Hedenborg White

MAGICK & HERMETICISM

SSOTBME Revised: An Essay on Magic by Ramsey Dukes
Initiation into Hermetics by Franz Bardon

QABALAH

A Garden of Pomegranates by Israel Regardie

Chicken Qabalah of Rabbi Lamed Ben Clifford: Dilettante's Guide to What You Do and Do Not Need to Know to Become a Qabalist by Lon Milo DuQuette

The Eight Temples Meditation Project by Rawn Clark

TAROT

Book of Thoth by Aleister Crowley

Understanding Aleister Crowley's Thoth Tarot: New Edition by Lon Milo Duquette

Seventy-Eight Degrees of Wisdom by Rachel Pollack

ALCHEMY

Practical Alchemy: A Guide to the Great Work by Brian Cotnoir

Alchemy: An Introduction to the Symbolism and the Psychology by Marie-Louise Franz

SPIRITS & GRIMOIRES

Consorting with Spirits: Your Guide to Working with Invisible Allies by Jason Miller

The Lesser Key of Solomon edited by Joseph H Peterson

Arbatel: Concerning the Magic of Ancients edited by Joseph H Peterson

The Book of Abramelin: A New Translation compiled and edited by George Dehn[32]

Geosophia: The Argo of Magic by Jake Stratton-Kent

POST-THELEMA

The Dark Lord: H P Lovecraft, Kenneth Grant and the Typhonian Tradition in Magic by Peter Levenda

Rites of the Mummy: The K'rla Cell and the Secret Key to Liber AL by Jeffrey D Evans and Peter Levenda

Maat Magick: A Guide to Self-Initiation by Nema

---

[32] This is the latest edition available, and it differs substantially by the one by Mathers and Crowley. By all means we should always strive to use more recent scholarship when possible!

The Horus Maat Lodge: The Grimoire of a PanAeonic Magickal Tribe by
The Inner Council of the HML

SORCERY

*The Grimoire of The Forty Servants: The Complete Guide to the Magick
and Divination System* by Tommie Kelly

Six Ways: Approaches & Entries for Practical Magic by Aidan Wachter

Weaving Fate: Hypersigils, Changing the Past, & Telling True Lies by
Aidan Wachter

Liber Null & Psychonaut: Revised and Expanded Edition by Peter J.
Carroll

Prime Chaos: Adventures in Chaos Magic, 3rd Revised Edition by Phil
Hine

Condensed Chaos: An Introduction to Chaos Magic by Phil Hine

YOGA & TANTRA

Pranayama by Gregor Maehle

*Tantra Illuminated: The Philosophy, History, and Practice of a Timeless
Tradition* by Christopher D Wallis

Tantric Temples: Eros and Magic in Java by Peter Levenda

A Chakra & Kundalini Workbook by Jonn Mumford

GNOSTICISM & ROSICRUCIANISM

Gnostic Philosophy by Tobias Churton

Invisibles: The True History of the Rosicrucians by Tobias Churton

Alois Mailander: A Rosicrucian Remembered by Samuel Robinson

The Gnostic Gospels by Elaine Pagels

AFTERWORD

My magic has always been of the bruised margins. Dole desperation, the necessary wardings when squatting. Blood and dust workings.

While wading through that thick cloud of uncritical biases, which is being a teenager, I took against ceremonial magic. My reasoning – as little as there was of it – focused on the way malarkey with swords and capes excluded those who could not afford such things. I was also instinctually against what I interpreted as an obsession with status and hierarchy. Most of all, I disliked its rampant obfuscation.

Those things still rankle me.

My magical heroes were discovered in comic books, zines and the places I walked. My magical heroes were John Constantine, Phil Hine and cunning folk, all the crow doctors of an Essex childhood. Peasant and punk magics at my core, I'm still cigarette smoke sigils, iron goggles and 21-pepper rum.

Of course I read Crowley. He was so soaked into the history of modern magic and pop culture it seemed like an act of wilful ignorance to avoid his texts. Yet around those texts, a toxic miasma of bastard claimants to legacy.

Approaching Thelema, you felt like a mythic knight hacking their way not through thorned hedge but swathes of nodding fans and gatekeepers while trying to get to the heart of any worthwhile knowledge. A landscape filled with iteration after iteration of pecking order pisspuffinry, deliberate befuddling and exclusion.

Not for me.

I will admit to also being turned away by some Crowley influenced. The grift of L Ron Hubbard, Anton LaVey and even Gerald Gardner provoked spontaneous nausea. The toad-cursing, brick-throwing, journalist-threatening antics of Kenneth Anger were hardly an enticement to reading of his muse. And let us not start on the sneering, preening and pontificating of Thelemites you often ran into in the late 1980s and 1990s. Narcissistic warbling is not new or peculiar to the first generation to grow up with the saturation of social media – as much as some old hands try to portray it as such.

Crowley himself, with his playing up to the ludicrous wickedest man in the world theatrics, was also not an inducement to return to the study of his work. The tale of Ian Fleming wanting to utilize him to debrief Rudolf Hess (confirmed to me personally by Jon Pertwee), but the Admiralty refusing due to his reputation seemed emblematic of his self-lacerating tactics. Wisdom obscured by the din of outer noise. The extra k as lens of mud.

Yet if my punk and peasant approach has taught me anything, it is to respect and use what works. Adopting tools that assist in actual doing, navigation by fundamental truths. Beyond their own versions of befogging, the way of many cunning folk was a blurring beyond the meaningless labels of high and low magic on a path of achieving through action.

Which is why I like this book. It is a text of performing, not pontificating. It bravely refuses to be obscurist. While Marco could have played games of *I-know-more-than-you*, there is none of it here. Instead, in an age of *witch grift*, here is a manual of *witch graft*. You have just devoured something that gives you what you need to know about Thelema and much of magick but has not been afraid to tell you that there's going to be work. A bloody awful lot of work.

This is a book on the occult that trusts its readers to be shown what is often hidden – a much rarer thing than it should be.

In London pubs, across many magic circles left by glasses of Guinness, Marco and I have often discussed providing ladders and ramps out of the predatory pits of those exploiting new students to the subject. This is not only him manifesting one of those ladders. It is a signposting of things to come.

Marco has provided a burning of armchairs, not of books. You've been given a kick up the arse to be magical, not to navel-gaze. You have a map of walls to climb over and traps to avoid. Use it.

Be imaginative. Be as willing to be inspired by obvious fictions of comic books as you are by the raw wonders of the world. Engage. Experiment. Observe. Most of all – *do!* The basics performed across decades make great magicians. The basics combined with expansive imagining create magicians who inspire others.

My way forward is to continue to dance with the *genii locorum*, to establish embassies with the enfolding otherworlds. My magics are about relationships. By turns, the path I walk may be quest, pilgrimage, or slog through the mire in a sinking world. I'll stay a creature of the margins and marches. My resistance will always be re-enchantment.

My way most likely will be entirely different to yours. Good.

In the time to come, I hope to learn from some of you who take this text and do things with it. Extraordinary things. Magical things.

You no longer have the excuse of not knowing how to do them.

David Southwell

ACKNOWLEDGEMENTS

My heartfelt thanks go to:

Jessica, for providing true companionship and love when I thought it was all gone.

Mars Neumann, for the invaluable help with graphics and design. You can find him online at: www.adventuresofamagus.com.

Peter Grandstaff, for the extra set of eyes at the proofread stage.

All the patrons, students, and seekers at the **Magick Without Tears** online community for their sincere support through good and bad times. Without them, this book would have never seen the light of the day.

The members of Ecclesia Gnostica Universalis in Anglia, for keeping alive the flame when it's darkest out there.

Steve Marshall for providing much-needed feedback with the book's manuscript, and telling me to tone it down – just a little. I definitely need that reminder more often than I like to admit.

Michael Staley for permission to use the drawing of LAM.

These fellow magical authors, magicians, esoteric connoisseurs, and heretics who provided inspiration, feedback, or both: Peter Levenda, David Southwell and Hookland, Clive Harper, Michael Bertiaux, Francesco Dimitri, Christina Oakley-Harrington and Treadwell's Books, Phil Hine, Stefania and the Helgi's crew, John Rogers, Rodney Orpheus, Meredith Graves, Giulia Turolla, Jason Miller, Gerald Del Campo, Tommie Kelly, Spud Murphy, Jason Mendel, Alexis Mincolla, Lon Milo DuQuette, Bishop Harber, Rawn Clark, Nathan Paul Isaac and the Penny Royal Podcast crew, Greg and Dana Newkirk and the Hellier phenomenon, Ashley Ryan, Pythian Priestess, Vanth Spiritwalker, Jason Augustus Newcomb, Alan

Moore, Grant Morrison, Robert Anton Wilson, Israel Regardie, Kenneth Grant, Zivorad Slavinski, Nema Andahadna, Linda Falorio, Alobar Greywalker, and last but surely not least, Aleister Crowley.

This book is dedicated to all of those still searching,
and that will endure till the end.
Because in the end there is nothing left to endure.

THE EXPERIENCE
CONTINUES ON THE NET

MULTIMEDIA LINKS

Scan the **QR code** or go to the URL below to access a series of multimedia files that enhance and give examples of the practices in the book.

marcovisconti.org/multimedia

MAGICK WITHOUT TEARS ONLINE

If you want to dive deeper into these practices, or if you have questions on any of them, join us at **Magick Without Tears** online at: *magick.marcovisconti.org*

You will find even more lessons, articles, weekly livestreams, seminars, and the opportunity to book one-on-one mentorship sessions with me directly.

INDEX

Note. Information in tables is indicated by page numbers in **bold**, in diagrams and illustrations by page numbers in *italics*.